PROUDLER FAMILY HISTORY

By Karen and Graham Proudler

Second Publication in Great Britain in 2013 by
Karen & Graham Proudler
Forge Cottage
Field Farm
Aston Lane
Shardlow
Derbyshire DE72 2GX
England

Cover picture:
Ann MERRIN (1842-1883)
Picture taken 1861
Ann died in childbirth
Ann is the maternal ancestor of many male lines of Derbyshire PROUDLERS

INDEX

INTRODUCTION

Everyone with the PROUDLER name is related and descends from one couple: Joseph PROUDLER (1762-1840) and Martha BLADEN (1763-1844) who were married on 23rd February 1786 in Shropshire. We visited Shrewsbury Record Office to view the original parish register and a transcript of the entry follows:

> **Joseph PROUDLER and Martha BLADEN both of this**
> **Parish were married by Banns this 23rd day of February**
> **in the Year One Thousand Seven Hundred and Eighty-Six**
> **by me Thomas OLIVER Curate.**
> **This marriage was solemnized between us Jo.PROUDLER**
> **(his mark) Martha BLADEN (her mark).**
> **In the presence of: Thomas PICKEN and John PLIMER.**

The marriage took place at All Saints Church, Wellington, Shropshire.[1]

No baptism record has ever been found for Joseph though his age was recorded on his death certificate.

Over a period of time, it was possible to piece together Joseph's family and their movements.

Prior to Joseph, the family name was PROUDLEY. Joseph's father Peter was born with the Proudley surname in High Ercall in Shropshire, but after marriage moves away from the area and that is where the spelling of the name changes to PROUDLER.

Everyone with the Proudler name can trace their ancestral line back to Joseph and Martha. Very few Proudlers remained in Shropshire; the main branches moved away to the West Midlands in 1833, Middlesbrough in 1870 and Derbyshire in 1890.

Due to restrictions imposed by the Data Protection Act 1998, information on living relations has been limited.

---

[1] Present-day All Saints Church Wellington was built in 1790 (after Joseph and Martha PROUDLER's marriage). The earlier medieval church they married in was located on the lawn just in front of the present one. In 1786, at the time of their marriage, the old medieval church was in bad shape; it had been very heavily damaged during the Civil War era and was in an almost derelict condition at that time.

From Proudley to Proudler ....

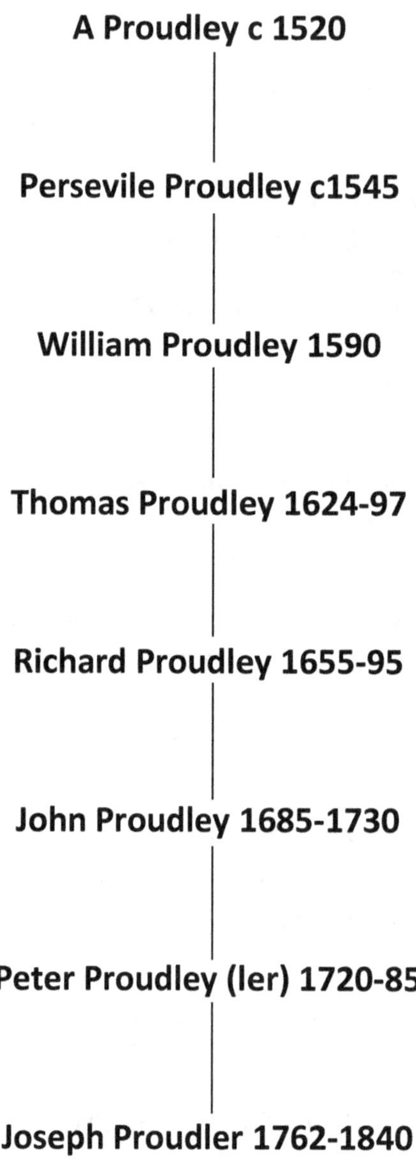

Earliest PROUDLER Ancestors

The first mention of Proudleys in the parish registers is at Martin Hussingtree in Worcester, then later at Old Swinford where they remained for some time. Much later, at the time of the English Civil War with all the disruption that would have caused, that is the time when at least one branch of this family cross over the county border into Shropshire. Some Wills have been located as follows:

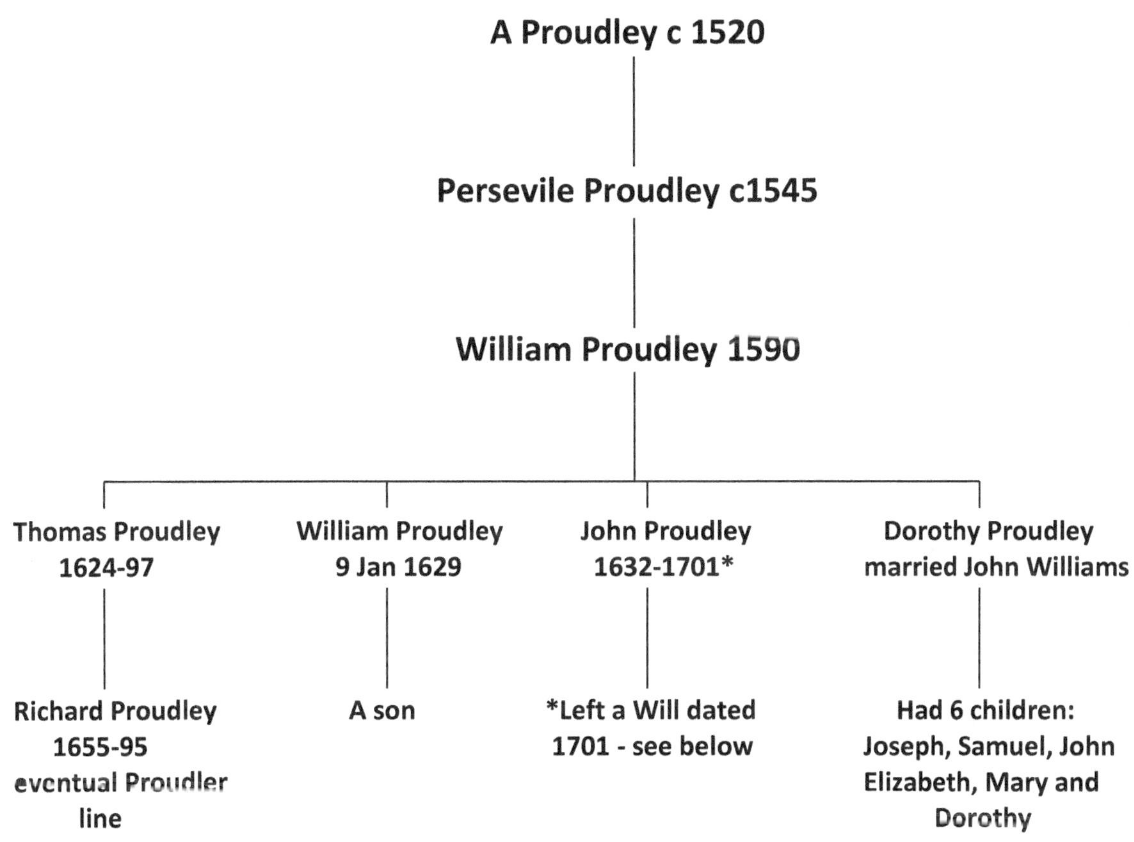

Transcript of the Will of William TEESE (husband of Mary PROUDLEY, widow of Richard PROUDLEY), dated 1720

In the name of God Amen, I William TEESE of Walton of the Club in the county of Salop being of sound and perfect mind and memory do make and ordain this my last Will and testament in manner and form following. First I commit my soul into the hands of Almighty God hoping through the merit of my saviour Jesus Christ to have full and free pardon of all my sins and to inherit eternal life and my body I commit to the earth to be decently buried at the discretion of my executrix hereafter named as to the disposal of my tempral goods cattel and chattels money credits and reversions to my dear wife Mary TEESE whom I make sole executrix of this my last will and testament now revoking all former wills heretofore made by me in witness whereof I hereunto put my hand and seal this twelfth day of September in the year of our Lord One Thousand Seven Hundred and Twenty. Witnessed b y Richard BLAKEWAY, Richard Church Signed (mark of) William TEESE

Inventory:

4 Cowes	2:00:00
Three little heffers	6:00:00
Sheep, worth	2:00:00
Swine, one sow and four pigs	1:10:00
In the house	0:05:00
In the chamber over the house and in the chamber upstairs	0:15:00
Brass and pewter of all sorts	0:10:00
Bedding withal belonging to house	0:15:00
Wooden ware of all sorts	4:00:00
Implements of husbandry of all sorts	1:00:00
His wearing apparel	0:05:00
All things unseen and forgotten	0:02:06
TOTAL	19:14:06

Transcription of both Wills (of difficult hand-writing) by Arthur Proudley - with thanks

The second Will is of John Proudley (cousin to Richard Proudley above):-

Will of John PROUDLEY, dated 23rd January 1701

In the name of God Amen the three and twentieth day of January in the Year of Our Lord One Thousand Seven Hundred and One. I John PROUDLEY of the parish of Old Swinford in the County of Worcester, tailor, being sick and weak but of perfect mind and memory praise be God for this I do make and ordain this my last will and testament in manner and form following. Viz, first I bequeath my soul into the hands of Almighty God my maker hoping that through the meritous death and resurrection of Jesus Christ my only saviour and redeemer to receive free pardon and forgiveness of all my sins and as for my body to be buried in such Christian burial as to my executor hereafter named shall think fit and as conferring such worldly goods chattels and cattel which it hath pleased God from above my desert to bestow on me. I do give and divide the same in manner and form following. First I will that all such debts and debtors in conscience am bound to pay to any manner of person or persons be fully satisfied and paid. Item I give unto my sister Dorothy the wife of John WILLIAMS twenty pounds being in the hands of Richard BIBB of Old Swinford aforesaid to be paid her the said Dorothy by four pounds per annum till the said twenty pounds be paid. Item I give to Dorothy the daughter of the aforesaid John WILLIAMS and Dorothy his wife five pounds. Item I give to Mary WILLIAMS my niece five pounds. Item I give to Elizabeth WILLIAMs sister to the said Mary WILLIAMS five pounds. Item I give to John WILLIAMS the son of John WILLIAMS and Dorothy his wife forty shillings. Item I give to Samuel WILLIAMS brother of the said John WILLIAMS the younger twenty shillings. Item I give to Margery PROUDLY the daughter of my brother Thomas PROUDLEY deceased twenty shillings. Item I give to Bridget WALL my niece now or later of Chaddesley Corbett five pounds. Item I give to the son of my brother William PROUDLY if living five pounds. Item I give to Joseph WILLIAMS my nephew whom I make and ordain to be the sole executor of this my last will and testament and in case any cost should be in getting my money which is now due to me so that the legacies afore bequested should amount to more with funeral expenses and proving the will according to the laws of the realm my will and desire is that every legatee before mentioned shall abate out of his or her legacy what shall justly be proved by my executor to be their share abated out of their legacy as aforesaid and desire Richard BIBB and Robert BARWELL, both of the parish of Old Swinford in the county of Worcester to be overseers of this my last will and testament desiring my executor to give them a pair of gloves apiece for their pains after my decease and desire them the said Richard and Robert BARWELL to be assisting to my executor and do their utmost to see this my will in everything fulfilled in witness thereof I the said John PROUDLEY to this my last will and testament, being wrote upon one sheet of paper, I hereunto put my hand and seal the day and year above written. Sealed, published and declared the last will and testament of the above named John PROUDLEY in the presence of .... Georg BARWELL; Richard BIBB, gent; Robert PAGET.
The mark of John WILLIAMS Gent; Signed John PROUDLY

MOVEMENT OF THE EARLIEST PROUDLEY FAMILIES

The earliest Worcester Lay Subsidy (tax records) shows the presence of:

.... De Ricardo le PROUDLE (of Northwyk) Worcester, and
.... De Willielmo le PROUDE (of Stonehall) Worcester

These early tax records date from 1280, 1346 and 1358 and this may well be the origin of the eventual Proudley and Proudler names.

c.1280	Worcester	Northwyk and Stonehall	De Ricardo le PROUDE, and De Willielmo le PROUDE
1578	Worcester	Martin Hussingtree	*(PROUDLEY)*
1580-1627	Worcester	Holt	Bapt of Joyce PROUDLEY
1623-1752	Worcester	Old Swinford	Mar of Will PROUDLEY/Perk
1631	Worcester	Rock	Bapt of Richard PROUDLEY
1637	Wales	Montgomery	Will of Evan PROUDLEY*
1644	Worcester	Kidderminster	Bapt of Ann PROUDLEY
1663	Derbyshire	Clowne	Mar of Will PROUDLEY1666
	Shropshire	Caynham	Mar of Thomas PROUDLEY
1676	Shropshire	Roddington	Mar of John PROUDLEY
1678	Shropshire	Whittington	Bapt of Richard PROUDLEY
1682	Shropshire	High Ercall (Walton)	Mar of Richard PROUDLEY
1699	Staffs	Kinver	Mar of Mary PROUDLEY
1702	Worcester	Chaddesley Corbett	Bapt of John PROUDLEY
1710	Hampshire	Romsey	Mar of John PROUDLEY
1711	Kent	Strood	Mar of A PROUDLEY
1721	Lincolnshire	Goxhill	Mar of John PROUDLEY
1739	Sussex	Westbourne	Bapt of Will PROUDLEY
1749	Yorkshire	Cottingham	Bapt of John PROUDLEY
1750s	**Shropshire**	**Wrockwardine Wood**	*(name evolves to PROUDLER)*
1766	Devon	Tiverton	
1783	Surrey		
1792	Hampshire	Portsea	
1865	Liverpool		

** A copy of Evan Proudley's Will follows:*

PROUDLEYs in Montgomeryshire, Wales
connected to PROUDLER ancestry

Prior to one or two branches of PROUDLEYs moving away from Worcester, across the county border, into Shropshire – (abt 1660s), a branch appears in Montgomeryshire, Wales (prior to 1630s). Although another county and, indeed, country – it is a short distance away only and it seems highly likely that this branch also originates in Worcester. There is also evidence of at least one link between the Montgomery PROUDLEYs and those in Shropshire. Viz: "8 May 1704 marriage of Richard PROWDLEY of Guilsfield and Mary JONES of Whittington". Source St Asaph Vol II, parts 2-3, Whittington. (Guilsfield is exactly where the Montgomery PROUDLEYs were located and Whittington is in Shropshire).

Earliest evidence of PROUDLEYs in Montgomery (Wales) commences with the Will of Evan PROUDLEY, dated 1636/7 (see below) and, in combination with the Penstrowed Parish Registers (which date from 1629), it is possible to sketch an outline of this branch and it is probable that the significant lines of PROUDLEY descendants in Wales may, in time, be traced back to this one family:

Will of Evan PROWDLEY (1636)

Defuncti probatum 10 die Julij 1637 Penystrowed
In dei nomine Amen, the xvjth daye of Julij 1636.

I, Evan PROWDLEY, of the p[ar]ish of Penstrowed in the county of Montgom[er]y and dyocs of Bangor, beinge sicke in bodye but of good and perfect memorie, laude and prayes be to God, doe make this my last will and testament in maner and forme following. First I commit my soule to the Almightie God my saviour and redeemer and my bodye to be buried according to Christian burial.
Item, I give toward the rep[ar]acion of the churche of Penstrowed ijs and also I give iijs to be distributed between the poore of the p[ar]ishe according to the appointment of my executor.
Item, I give to my sone Richard one three yere ould heifer. I give to my sonne Edward one three yere ould heifer. I give to my sonne Oliver one three yere old heifer. I give to my daughter Elizabeth one three yere oulde heifer, alsoe I give to my daughter Marye one three yere old heifer and alsoe I give and bequeath fiftie sheepe to be equallie devided between my five children at the four yeres ende and if any of the children shall happen to dye within the space of four yeres the p[ar]te of that child dying of ..... sheepe is to be equallie devyded between the other foure children and alsoe I give and bequeath to my five forenamed children twentie shillings a peece to be payd as abovesaid. And alsoe I give and bequeath to Anne one of the daughters of Olliver SWINDELL, one lamb. And alsoe I doe give and bequeath all my goods, cattells, and chattels, moveable and unmoveable and unbequethed whatsoever to Jane my wedded wife, whom I doe nominate and appoint my executor of this my last will depts. Owinge to the testator by specialtie upon Richard SYRE viijt. Depts without specialties upon Evan JONES five pounds to be paid at Michaelmas next and thease sythens maye last past debts to the testator upon Willm BAYLY p[ar]sone of Penstrewed xxxs, dewe by an adwarde made by Mr Alexander GRIFFITH, Thomas JENYNGS and others, whereof Mr GRIFFITH undertook to paye the same.
[Next page – only a portion remains]
Six and twentie sheepe at bargayne [with]
Mori s ap OWEN of Llanunocke to be delived sheering tyme next viz at maye next Thus
I doe nominate and appoint Thomas JENYNGS, Richard JENYNGS and Olliver SWINDALL overseers of this my last will and testament.

Witness [e]s at this present will and testamt
Thomas JENYNGS, Richard JENYNGS, Oliver SWINDELL, Tho. JONES

The following is an outline of Evan's family

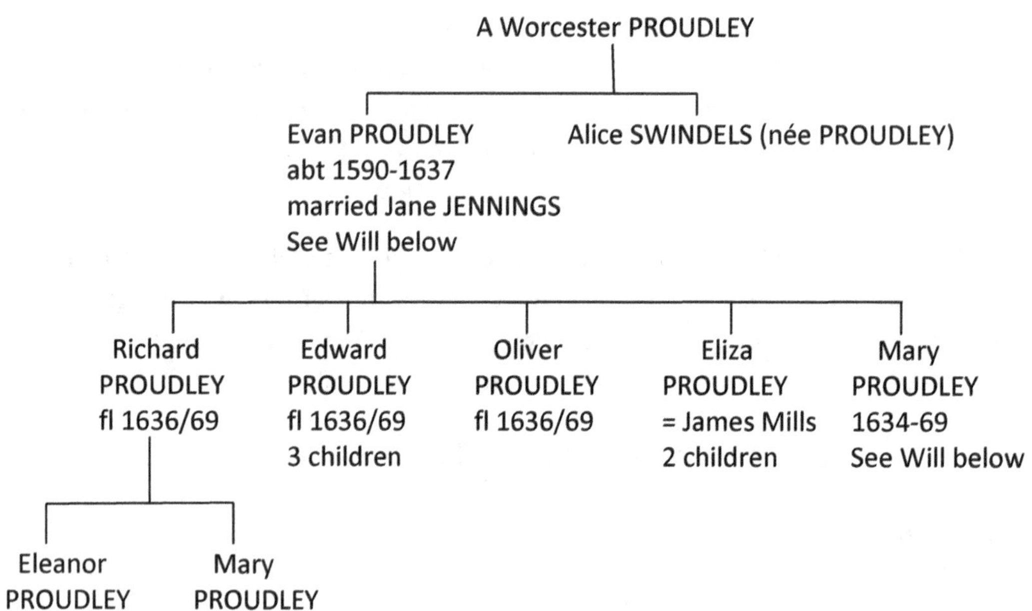

PENSTROWED PARISH RECORDS (WALES) FROM 1629
1629   Baptism of Elizabeth, daughter of Evan PROUDLEY and Jane JENNING
1631   Burial of Elizabeth, daughter of Evan PROUDLEY and Jane JENNING, buried 13th December
1634   Baptism of Mary, daughter of Evan PROUDLEY and Jane JENNING, baptised 27th January
1640   Baptism of Richard, son of John PROUDLEY and Elinor JONES, baptism 21st January
1640   Marriage of John PROUDLEY and Helena (Cooper?), 12th November
1631   Burial of Elizabeth PROUDLEY, 13th December
1631   Burial of Richard PROUDLEY, 13th February
1632   Burial of Elizabeth PROUDLEY, widow, 23rd September
1636   Burial of Evan PROUDLEY, July.

EARLY PROUDLEY GENEALOGY

The following genealogy shows the first records we have of Proudleys in Worcester through to their arrival in Shropshire in the 1600s. The direct line of Proudler ancestors is highlighted in bold.

Descendants of ? Proudley

Generation No. 1

1. ?[1] PROUDLEY was born Abt. 1520.
Child of A PROUDLEY is:
2.　　　　i.　**PERSEVILE[2] PROUDLEY, b. Abt. 1545, Worcester.**

Generation No. 2

2. PERSEVILE[2] PROUDLEY (?[1]) was born about 1545 in Worcester. He married EMMA PATRICK August 4, 1576 in Holt, Worcester. She was born May 1540 in Holt, Worcester, and died March 2, 1613/14.
Source: Parish Registers of Holt, Worcs

Children of PERSEVILE PROUDLEY and EMMA PATRICK are:
　　　　　i.　ALICE[3] PROUDLEY, b. Abt. 1577; m. OLIVER SWINDELLS.
3.　　　ii.　DOROTHY PROUDLEY, b. October 19, 1578, Martin Hussingtree, Worcs.
4.　　　iii.　EVAN PROUDLEY, b. 1590; d. 1637.
　　　　　iv.　JOYCE PROUDLEY, b. 1580, Holt, Worcester.
　　　　　v.　AGNES PROUDLEY, b. December 25, 1583, Holt, Worcester.
　　　　　vi.　PERSIDA PROUDLEY, b. December 4, 1586, Holt, Worcester; d. June 10, 1611.
5.　　**vii.**　**WILLIAM PROUDLEY, b. 1590, Holt, Worcester.**

Generation No. 3

3. DOROTHY[3] PROUDLEY *(PERSEVILE[2], ?[1])* was born October 19, 1578 in Martin Hussingtree, Worcs. She married JONATHAN SPARKE Abt. 1595. He was born Abt. 1570.
More About JONATHAN SPARKE: John Sparke was born 25 Apr 1569 and baptised 5 Mar 1579. He had a son Richard Masfield bapt 7 Jan 1588. A Humphrey Spark (churchwarden) who could be brother to John.

Child of DOROTHY PROUDLEY and JONATHAN SPARKE is:
6.　　　i.　JONE PROUDLEY, b. March 30, 1604; d. August 18, 1685.

4. EVAN[3] PROUDLEY *(PERSEVILE[2], ?[1])* was born 1590, and died 1637. He married JANE JENNINGS.

Children of EVAN PROUDLEY and JANE JENNINGS are:
7.　　　i.　RICHARD PROUDLEY.
　　　　　ii.　EDWARD PROUDLEY: Alive in 1636 and 1669, mentioned in wills
　　　　　iii.　OLIVER PROUDLEY: Alive in 1636 and 1669, mentioned in wills
　　　　　iv.　ELIZABETH PROUDLEY, d. Aft. 1663; m. JAMES MILLER.
　　　　　v.　MARY PROUDLEY, b. January 27, 1633/34; d. 1669.

5. WILLIAM³ PROUDLEY *(PERSEVILE², ?¹)* **was born 1590** in Holt, Worcester. He married BRIDGET PERKES May 1, 1623 in Old Swinford, Worcs. She was born 1604.

Children of WILLIAM PROUDLEY and BRIDGET PERKES are:
8.   i.   **THOMAS PROUDLEY, b. February 27, 1623/24,** Old Swinford, Worcs; d. April 12, 1697, Old Swinford, Worcs.
    ii. JONE PROUDLEY, b. March 9, 1626/27, Old Swinford, Worcs. Died: Infant.
9.   iii. WILLIAM PROUDLEY, b. January 9, 1628/29, Old Swinford, Worcs.
    iv. JOHN PROUDLEY, b. September 29, 1632, Old Swinford, Worcs; d. January 1700/01, Old Swinford, Worcs. More About JOHN PROUDLEY: Nts: Will available Occ: Tailor
10.   v. BRIDGET PROUDLEY, b. October 3, 1636, Old Swinford, Worcs.
11.   vi. DOROTHY PROUDLEY, b. April 12, 1645, Old Swinford, Worcs.

Generation No. 4

6. JONE⁴ PROUDLEY *(DOROTHY³, PERSEVILE², ?¹* was born March 30, 1604, and died August 18, 1685.
Children of JONE PROUDLEY are:
12.   i. JOANNE PROUDLEY, b. January 7, 1625/26, Holt, Worcester.
    ii. RICHARD PROUDLEY, b. January 23, 1630/31, Rock, Worcester; m. ELIZABETH ARTHUR, 1670, Montgomery, Wales; b. Abt. 1635.

7. RICHARD⁴ PROUDLEY *(EVAN³, PERSEVILE²,?¹)* He married ?.
More About RICHARD PROUDLEY: Alive in 1636 and 1669 (on wills)
Children of RICHARD PROUDLEY and ? are:
    i. ELEANOR PROUDLEY.
    ii. MARY PROUDLEY.

8. THOMAS⁴ PROUDLEY *(WILLIAM³, PERSEVILE², ?¹)* was born February 27, 1623/24 in Old Swinford, Worcs, and died April 12, 1697 in Old Swinford, Worcs. He married ?.
More About THOMAS PROUDLEY: Loc: Old Swinford, Worcs

Children of THOMAS PROUDLEY and ? are:
13.   i. THOMAS PROUDLEY, b. March 1, 1649/50, Old Swinford, Worcs; d. 1675.
14.   ii. WILLIAM PROUDLEY, b. January 29, 1651/52, Old Swinford, Worcs.
    iii. SAMUEL PROUDLEY, b. December 23, 1654, Old Swinford, Worcs.
15.   iv. **RICHARD PROUDLEY, b. Abt. 1655, Old Swinford, Worcs;** d. May 1, 1695, High Ercall, Shropshire.
    v. JOHN PROUDLEY, b. December 3, 1656, Old Swinford, Worcs; d. 1656, Old Swinford, Worcs.
    vi. JOHN PROUDLEY, b. February 7, 1657/58, Old Swinford, Worcs; d. February 7, 1709/10, Roddington, Salop; m. ANN LLOYD, April 23, 1676, Roddington, Salop; d. February 11, 1709/10, Roddington, Salop. Src: Roddington par. reg.
    vii. MARGERY PROUDLEY, b. April 11, 1658, Old Swinford, Worcs; m. HENRY ADDENBROOKE, November 5, 1702, Chaddesley Corbett, Worcs.
    viii. MARY PROUDLEY, b. December 13, 1663, Old Swinford, Worcs; m. RICHARD FEREDAY, May 29, 1699, Kinver, Staffs.
    ix. BRIDGET PROUDLEY, b. May 20, 1666, Old Swinford, Worcs; d. August 25, 1672.

9. WILLIAM[4] PROUDLEY *(WILLIAM[3], PERSEVILE[2], ?[1])* was born January 9, 1628/29 in Old Swinford, Worcs. He married (1) ELINOR.   He married (2) ROSAMUND WHITE November 5, 1663 in Clowne, Derbyshire.

Children of WILLIAM PROUDLEY and ELINOR are:

	i.	ANNE PROUDLEY, b. January 27, 1643/44, Kidderminster; m. CHRISTOPHER HUMPHRIES, April 15, 1672, St Mary's Kidderminster, Worcester.
	ii.	ELINOR PROUDLEY, b. August 23, 1651, Kidderminster.
16.	iii.	THOMAS PROUDLEY, b. 1660.
17.	iv.	WILLIAM PROUDLEY, b. 1662, Clowne, Derbys.

10. BRIDGET[4] PROUDLEY *(WILLIAM[3], PERSEVILE[2], ?[1])* was born October 3, 1636 in Old Swinford, Worcs. She married (1) M WALL, she married (2) THOMAS BRIDGE 1666 in Old Swinford, Worcs.

Child of BRIDGET PROUDLEY and M WALL is:

     i.   BRIDGET WALL, b. Unknown, Chaddesley Corbett. Receives bequest at Uncle John's will dated 1701.

11. DOROTHY[4] PROUDLEY *(WILLIAM[3], PERSEVILE[2], ?[1])* was born April 12, 1645 in Old Swinford, Worcs. She married JOHN WILLIAMS abt. 1670 in Old Swinford, Worcs.

Children of DOROTHY PROUDLEY and JOHN WILLIAMS are:

     i.   DOROTHY WILLIAMS, b. Abt. 1675; d. Aft. 1701. Receives bequest at Uncle John's will dated 1701

     ii.   ELIZABETH WILLIAMS, b. Abt. 1677. Receives bequest at Uncle John's will dated 1701

     iii.   JOHN WILLIAMS, b. Abt. 1679; m. DOROTHY. Receives bequest at Uncle John's will dated 1701

     iv.   SAMUEL WILLIAMS, b. Abt. 1681.

     v.   JOSEPH WILLIAMS, b. Abt. 1683. More About JOSEPH WILLIAMS: Receives bequest at Uncle John's will dated 1701.

Generation No. 5

12. JOANNE[5] PROUDLEY *(JONE[4], DOROTHY[3], PERSEVILE[2], ?[1])* was born January 7, 1625/26 in Holt, Worcester.

Children of JOANNE PROUDLEY are:

     i.   THOMAS PROUDLEY, b. September 8, 1655, Holt, Worcester.

     ii.   GILBERT PROUDLEY, b. October 27, 1667, Holt, Worcester

13. THOMAS[5] PROUDLEY *(THOMAS[4], WILLIAM[3], PERSEVILE[2], ?[1])* was born March 1, 1649/50 in Old Swinford, Worcs, and died 1675. He married MARGARET JONES July 12, 1666 in Caynham, Salop. More About THOMAS PROUDLEY: Records say ...death of a Thomas Proudley "a poore man".

Child of THOMAS PROUDLEY and MARGARET JONES is:

     i.   JOSEPH PROUDLEY, b. October 31, 1675; d. 1675, Old Swinford, Worcs.

14. WILLIAM[5] PROUDLEY *(THOMAS[4], WILLIAM[3], PERSEVILE[2], ?[1])* was born January 29, 1651/52 in Old Swinford, Worcs. He married ?.

Child of WILLIAM PROUDLEY and ? is:

18.   i.   RICHARD PROUDLEY, b. 1678, Guilsfield, Wales.

15. RICHARD⁵ PROUDLEY *(THOMAS⁴, WILLIAM³, PERSEVILE², ?¹)* was born Abt. 1655 in Old Swinford, Worcs, and died May 1, 1695 in High Ercall, Shropshire. He married MARY CHIRME June 5, 1682 in High Ercall. She was born March 16, 1654/55 in High Ercall, Shropshire, and died 1720 in High Ercall, Shropshire. No baptism record found; pays church Rates in 1685 and 1694: On High Ercall par.reg described as "of Walton of the Club", High Ercall.
Children of RICHARD PROUDLEY and MARY CHIRME are:
19.   i.   RICHARD PROUDLEY, b. April 15, 1683, High Ercall, Shropshire.
20.   ii.   **JOHN PROUDLEY, b. October 26, 1685**, High Ercall, Shropshire; d. April 14, 1730, Walton, High Ercall, Shropshire.
21.   iii.   THOMAS PROUDLEY, b. November 19, 1688, High Ercall, Shropshire; d. May 5, 1766, High Ercall, Shropshire.
            iv.   SAMUEL PROUDLEY, b. April 23, 1691, High Ercall, Shropshire; d. August 10, 1699, High Ercall, Shropshire. THOMAS PROUDLEY *(WILLIAM⁴, WILLIAM³, PERSEVILE², ?¹)* was born 1660. He married ANN HILL June 17, 1685 in Kidderminster.

Child of THOMAS PROUDLEY and ANN HILL is:
22.   i.   THOMAS PROUDLEY, b. June 24, 1686, Kidderminster, Worcester.

17. WILLIAM⁵ PROUDLEY *(WILLIAM⁴, WILLIAM³, PERSEVILE², ?¹)¹* was born 1662 in Clowne, Derbys. He married ANN SPITTLEHOUSE November 19, 1682 in Clowne, Derbyshire.

Child of WILLIAM PROUDLEY and ANN SPITTLEHOUSE is:
            i.   ? PROUDLEY, b. 1682, Clowne, Derbys.

Generation No. 6

18. RICHARD⁶ PROUDLEY *(WILLIAM⁵, THOMAS⁴, WILLIAM³, PERSEVILE², ?¹)* was born 1678 in Guilsfield, Wales. He married MARY JONES April 1703 in Whittington, Salop.
Child of RICHARD PROUDLEY and MARY JONES is:
            i.   MARY PROUDLEY, b. 1705; m. RICHARD DOWLEY, August 28, 1736, St Chad, Staffs.

19. RICHARD⁶ PROUDLEY *(RICHARD⁵, THOMAS⁴, WILLIAM³, PERSEVILE², ?¹)* was born April 15, 1683 in High Ercall, Shropshire. He married (1) MARY PASCALL November 5, 1711 in High Ercall.   He married (2) ELIZABETH SUTTON February 13, 1712/13 in Upton Magna, Salop. She was born 1682.

Child of RICHARD PROUDLEY and MARY PASCALL is:
            i.   MARY PROUDLEY, b. November 28, 1712, Childs Ercall.

Child of RICHARD PROUDLEY and ELIZABETH SUTTON is:
           ii.   THOMAS PROUDLEY, b. May 15, 1717, Wellington.

20. JOHN⁶ PROUDLEY *(RICHARD⁵, THOMAS⁴, WILLIAM³, PERSEVILE², ?¹)* **was born October 26, 1685 in High Ercall, Shropshire,** and died April 14, 1730 in Walton, High Ercall, Shropshire. He married ANNE HASELDINE June 1, 1713 in High Ercall. She died August 22, 1729 in High Ercall, Shropshire. Parish register records he died in the township of Walton, High Ercall.

Children of JOHN PROUDLEY and ANNE HASELDINE are:

     i.   ANN PROUDLEY, b. April 8, 1714.

23.   ii. JOHN PROUDLEY, b. November 25, 1716, High Ercall, Shropshire; d. March 6, 1742/43, Walton, High Ercall, Shropshire.

24.   iii. **PETER PROUDLEY, b. July 3, 1720, High Ercall, Shropshire; d. April 3, 1785, Wrockwardine.**

21. THOMAS[6] PROUDLEY *(RICHARD[5], THOMAS[4], WILLIAM[3], PERSEVILE[2], ?[1])* was born November 19, 1688 in High Ercall, Shropshire, and died May 5, 1766 in High Ercall, Shropshire. He married SARAH RODENHURST September 22, 1712 in St Chads, Shrewsbury. She died January 17, 1759 in Walton, High Ercall, Shropshire. More About THOMAS PROUDLEY: Pays church Rates in 1735 and overseers rate in 1761. Nts: Referred to in H.E. par.reg. as being of Walton & at his burial described as "an 'hospital man".

Children of THOMAS PROUDLEY and SARAH RODENHURST are:

     i.   THOMAS PROUDLEY, b. November 17, 1713, High Ercall, Shropshire; d. December 11, 1735, Walton, High Ercall, Shropshire.

25.   ii. EDWARD PROUDLEY, b. September 28, 1717, High Ercall, Shropshire; d. July 10, 1778, High Ercall, Shropshire.

26.   iii. SARAH PROUDLEY, b. April 10, 1720, High Ercall, Shropshire; d. July 30, 1784, High Ercall, Shropshire.

     iv. MARY PROUDLEY, b. April 29, 1722, High Ercall, Shropshire; m. JOHN ARMSTRONG, April 8, 1738.

     v. WILLIAM PROUDLEY, b. October 23, 1726, High Ercall, Shropshire; d. June 20, 1729, Walton, High Ercall, Shropshire.

22. THOMAS[6] PROUDLEY *(THOMAS[5], WILLIAM[4], WILLIAM[3], PERSEVILE[2], ?[1])* was born June 24, 1686 in Kidderminster, Worcester. He married (1) ALICE DAWKES August 18, 1710 in Chaddesley Corbett, Worcs[1]. He married (2) SARA SCRIVEN 1726 in Kidderminster or Hartlebury.

Children of THOMAS PROUDLEY and ALICE DAWKES are:

27.   i.   SARAH[7] PROUDLEY, b. 1711.

     ii. THOMAS PROUDLEY, b. Abt. 1713.

Generation No. 7

23. JOHN[7] PROUDLEY *(JOHN[6], RICHARD[5], THOMAS[4], WILLIAM[3], PERSEVILE[2], ?[1])* was born November 25, 1716 in High Ercall, Shropshire, and died March 6, 1742/43 in Walton, High Ercall, Shropshire. He married MARY REECE October 17, 1736 in Stanton upon Hine Heath, Salop. She died June 12, 1771 in Walton, High Ercall, Shropshire. Nts: Referred to in the parish register as "John of The Oak"

Children of JOHN PROUDLEY and MARY REECE are:

     i.   ANN PROUDLEY, b. February 7, 1737/38

28.   ii. CHRISTIAN PROUDLEY, b. January 29, 1740/41.

     iii. ELIZABETH PROUDLEY, b. February 27, 1740/41; d. 1741, Walton, High Ercall, Shropshire

     iv. ELIZABETH PROUDLEY, b. November 20, 1743; m. GEORGE SMITH, December 3, 1763, Diddlebury, Salop. More About ELIZABETH PROUDLEY: She must have been born immediately after her father's death, as the records state she was "daughter of the Widow Proudley of The Oak" More About GEORGE SMITH: Nts: Witnesses at wedding: Edward Glace & John Cound.

Possible Origins of PROUDLEY
and PROUDLER Names

Surnames became necessary with the introduction by the Normans of national taxation to England in the form of the Poll Tax. Names and their spellings, varied by county and different pronunciations.

There are several suggestions as to where the Proudley surname originates; these are some ...

The PROUDLER surname evolves directly from the PROUDLEY surname and the earliest parish registers show that, prior to being in Shropshire, the PROUDLEYs were in Worcester in the 1500s. In Worcester, from the earliest time when surnames were becoming necessary and forming/settling – that is, the 1200s – there are instances of individuals referred to in Worcester as "le Proude" (Norman names). It is likely that the name evolved from the earliest records of Proudes – and that they were either entirely English in origin or, perhaps, that the family name originated in France (the low countries) from individuals who were relocated to England (possibly protestants forcibly removed, i.e. expelled from Catholic countries) arriving here at some point before this.

* * *

Another suggestion is that the name "Prowdley" means "Pruda's grove" or glade (taken from the Old English 7th Century personal name "Pruda") from "prud", poud and "leah", a glade in a wood, or grove. From the parish registers, there is a marriage of William Proudley and Bridgett Perkes recorded at Old Swinford, Worcestershire on May 1st, 1623. Also, the first recorded spelling of the family name is shown to be that of Dorithye Proudlye (christening) which was dated October 19th 1578, Martin Hussingtree, Worcestershire.

* * *

Recorded as Proud, Proude, Prout and the rare Proudlar, PROUDLER and Proudlor, this is an English medieval surname. It originated either as a nickname for a proud or haughty person. It is from the seventh century word "prut or prud", and it is said that as Prud it may have existed as a personal name in ancient times. As Proud the surname is said to be much associated with the county of Northumberland. Early examples of recordings include Orgar le Prude in the Calendar of Letter Books of the City of London in 1125. There is a Richard Prude of Shropshire in the records of the Knights Templar (Crusaders) in 1185, and a William Prute in the Pipe Rolls of Devonshire in the year 1207. The first recorded spelling of the family name is shown to be that of Toui Prude. This was dated 1033.

* * *

From A Dictionary of English Surnames. Oxford University Press. Authors Reaney & Wilson 1997. "Proudlove, PROUDLER: Thomas Prudelove 1289 AssCh. A nickname of TRUELOVE, TRUSLOVE". Legal documents and court cases are among the very few documents that survive the centuries. Most people didn't write at all then. The above authors scoured the oldest documents they could find to locate the first instance of a name being used. This is what they have listed under PROUDLER. A Proudlove descendant told me the above refers to a land dispute in Poynton in the year 1289. The Proudloves were, and still are, prevalent in the Chester area, amongst other areas. The AssCh referred to means the Assizes at Chester. Working on the sound of names, they have taken the above to be the first recorded instance of a name which evolved eventually to our own.

WHERE THE PROUDLER NAME BEGINS

So, we have explored the first six generations of Proudley ancestors and this now brings us to Peter Proudley (generation 7)- the man who is to move away from the High Ercall area of Shropshire towards Wrockwardine. The spelling of the name fluctuates for a time before finally settling as Proudler. Peter himself is born and married as Proudley, but buried in Wrockwardine as PROUDLER.

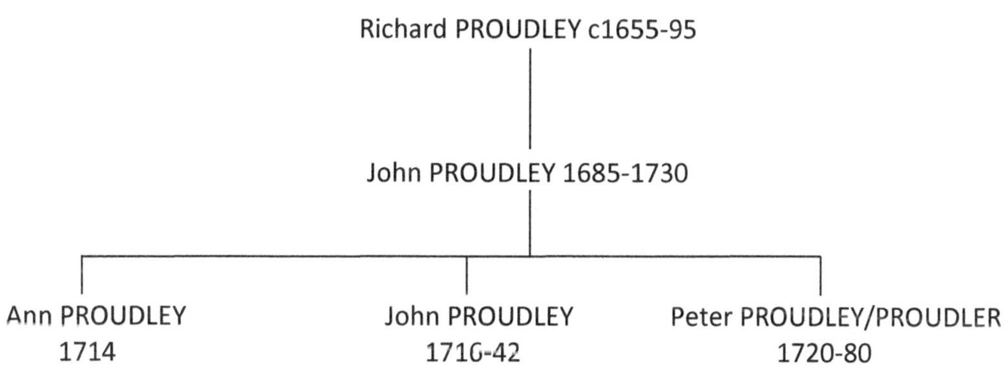

PETER[7] PROUDLEY *(JOHN[6], RICHARD[5], THOMAS[4], WILLIAM[3], PERSEVILE[2], ?[1])* was born July 3, 1720 in High Ercall, Shropshire[2], and died April 3, 1785 in Wrockwardine. He married ELIZABETH TALBOTT October 2, 1745 in High Ercall. She was born 1720, and died August 24, 1780 in Wrockwardine.

After marriage Peter moves away from High Ercall south-easterly and, as he does so, spelling of the name evolves to Proudlow (in Longford-by-Newport)[3], then later in Wrockwardine where the family settle in the mid-1700s, the Proudler name emerges. Peter and Elizabeth have eight children, but only the youngest son Joseph's line continues the family name.

---

[2] See Appendix 1-3 for parish register extracts
[3] See Appendix 4 - Poor Law Relief, Settlement Examinations for Longford-by-Newport

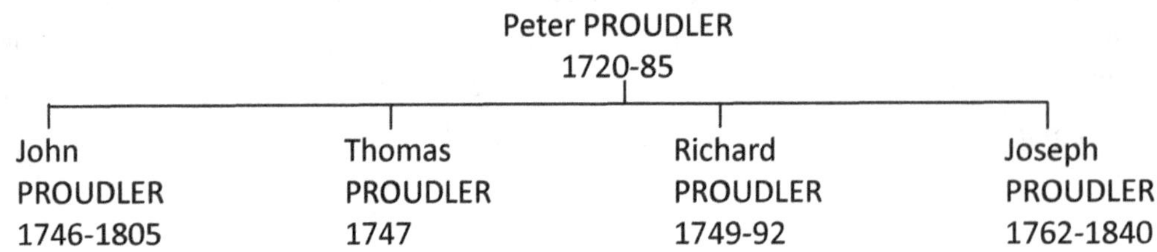

Children of PETER PROUDLEY and ELIZABETH TALBOTT are:

i. JOHN[8] PROUDLER, b. 1746; d. September 6, 1805, Wrockwardine; m. JANE.
ii. THOMAS PROUDLER, b. 1747, Eyton on the Weald Moors, Salop; d. 1755, Wrockwardine.
More About THOMAS PROUDLER: Nts: Died at Wrockwardine
iii. RICHARD PROUDLER/LEY/LOW, b. February 2, 1749/50, Longford-by-Newport, Salop;
d. July 23, 1792, Lilleshall.
iv. ELIZABETH PROUDLER, b. May 3, 1752, Wrockwardine [Wombridge]; m. RICHARD MATHEWS, December 28, 1775, All Saints Wellington.
v. ANN PROUDLAW, b. November 3, 1754, Wrockwardine; m. FRANCIS EVANS, January 14, 1778, Shifnal.
vi. MARY PROUDLER, b. Abt. 1756; d. 1763, Wrockwardine.
vii. SARAH PROUDLER, b. Abt. 1757; m. JOHN TAYLOR, 1781.
More About SARAH PROUDLER: Mar: 1781 Wellington All Saints
viii. JOSEPH PROUDLER, b. 1762; d. 1840, Wrockwardine, Salop. Married Martha Bladen.

A document was found concerning Richard that supports the fact that PROUDLER ancestors were PROUDLEYs, 'Settlement Examinations' (transcribed by members of the North East Telford Studies Group) shows Peter's son Richard (listed as spelling PROUDLOW) being in receipt of Poor Law Relief in 1783; his age being rounded down:

**P316/L/8/93. Dec 03., 1783. Examination of Richard PROUDLOW (X), age 30, wife
Ann, Children: Jane 5, Elizabeth 3, Richard inf. Born Pave Lane, Longford, Salop
lives at Wrockwardine Wood. High Ercall, his father's parish.**

On arrival in a parish, anyone requiring Poor Law Relief would be required to submit themselves to a Board for examination and, as part of that process, they were required to state where they had come from and what parish their family had previously lived in; so this document gives us confirmation of this family's movement from High Ercall to Wrockwardine in Shropshire.

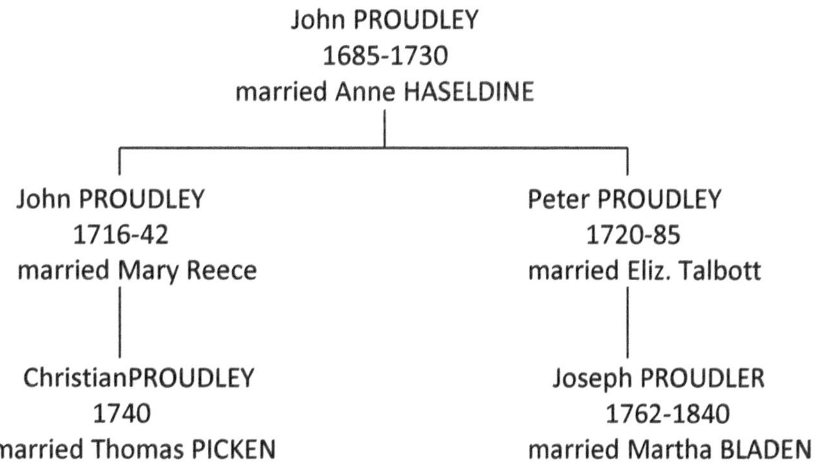

The above chart shows a further Proudley - Proudler connection: on the wedding certificate for Joseph Proudler and Martha Bladen: one of the witnesses at their wedding was Thomas PICKEN - who was married to Christian Proudley (Joseph's cousin)... Extract from St Chad's Parish Registers, Shropshire:

PROUDLEY, Christian marries Thomas PICKEN 8 July 1766

JOSEPH AND MARTHA PROUDLER

Peter 1720-85 may have been the first to be buried with the Proudler name, but it is with Joseph and Martha that the name, and its spelling, settle and become established.

JOSEPH PROUDLER, 1762-1840, Wrockwardine, Salop.

Joseph and his family moved away from Wrockwardine later after marriage to the Shifnal/Priorslee area. The area where Joseph and his family lived was called Snedshill Coppice.[4] Joseph PROUDLER's wife Martha (nee Bladen) is on the 1841 census (spelling Prowdler), aged 80 years, occupation school mistress, address Snedshill Coppice. Also, on the 1841 census, (probably living very close by) is Joseph and Martha's daughter-in-law, the widowed Mary PROUDLER (nee Cadwallader) still living at Snedshill Coppice with her children, including Sarah (the mother of all the Derbyshire PROUDLERs). The address for this same family by 1851 is just referred to as "Snedshill".

JOSEPH[8] **PROUDLER** *(PETER*[7] *PROUDLEY, JOHN*[6]*, RICHARD*[5]*, THOMAS*[4]*, WILLIAM*[3]*, PERSEVILL*[2]*, ?*[1]*)* was born 1762, and died 1840 in Wrockwardine, Salop. He married MARTHA BLADEN February 23, 1786 at All Saints, Wellington, Shropshire. She was born May 24, 1763 in Wellington, Shropshire, and died

---

[4] Snedshill Coppice has been developed over today but many of the small houses built in this area were blocks (barracks) built of brick for workers employed at the coalpits of Lilleshall – for the Earl Gower Company (later The Lilleshall Company). The Gower family (Dukes of Sutherland) were one of the richest in England at the time. These blocks of 12 single-storey houses had a wash house at each end, plus one in the centre. There were 27 dwellings at Waxhill Barracks and 67 dwellings at Donnington Barracks. These two barracks developed their own community identity and Donnington Barracks, in particular, was during 1842 the centre of huge industrial unrest. (British History Online – Lilleshall). The addresses where PROUDLERs lived was described as "Pains Lane" which, over a period of time, developed into the industrial hamlet we have today of St Georges. Snedshill Barracks was right next to Snedshill Coppice.*They have all now been demolished.

January 8, 1844 in Snedshill. Nts: Witnesses at wedding: Thomas Picken and John Plimer
Joseph's occupation: Labourer. Martha's occupation: Schoolmistress on the 1841 census.

Children of JOSEPH PROUDLER and MARTHA BLADEN are:
     i.   ELIZABETH[9] PROUDLER, b. 1786; d. 1820.
           More About ELIZABETH PROUDLER: Nts: Recorded as Bowdler on IGI.
           Src: Trench burial index
     ii.   ANN PROUDLAR, b. October 25, 1789; d. October 10, 1843, Shifnal, Salop.
     iii. SARAH PROUDLER, b. 1791; d. 1816.
           More About SARAH PROUDLER: Src: Snedshill burial index
     iv. JOHN PROUDLER, b. May 2, 1795, Shifnal, Shropshire; d. March 2, 1796, Shifnal, Shropshire,
           Priorslee Chapel.
           More About JOHN PROUDLER: Loc: Salop Source: Shifnal baptisms/Priorslee Chapel
     v.   THOMAS PROUDLER, b. March 5, 1797, Shifnal, Shropshire; d. August 16, 1835, Snedshill.
     vi. JOHN PROUDLER, b. 1800, Shifnal; d. June 20, 1860, Pensnett.
     vii. JOSEPH PROUDLER, b. 1805; d. 1808, Wombridge.
     viii. ALAN PROUDLER, b. 1806.

Joseph's death certificate says - cause of death: "decay of nature".

Of Joseph and Martha's children, it is their son John (1800-1860) who is the first to branch away from
Shropshire. He will move, around 1833, to Pensnett in the West Midlands and commence a Proudler
branch that is thriving there today. Proudlers in Swindon, Hartlepool and Canada can trace their origins
to this branch.

Son Thomas (1797-1835) does not leave Shropshire himself, but his son Thomas (1832-78) moves to
North Yorkshire around 1870 and commences another line of descent.

Daughter Sarah b. 1824 who has some illegitimate children (before marriage) - the eldest of whom,
David b.1852, will move to Derby about 1890 and settle the Proudler family in that county.

Son John 1829-1919 remains in Shropshire and present-day Proudlers (of whom there are few) descend
from him.

So, from this point onwards, the genealogy separates into the four branches:

       -      West Midlands Branch - from 1833

       -      Yorkshire/Durham Branch - from 1870

       -      Derbyshire Branch - from 1890

       -      Shropshire - to the present day

Descendants of John Proudler - son of Joseph

1   John Proudler b: 1800 in Shifnal d: June 20, 1860 in Pensnett
..   +Elizabeth Forgham b: 1804 m: May 9, 1825 in Wellington, Shropshire   d: October 22, 1886 in Stourbridge
.... 2 Joseph Proudler b: April 9, 1826 in Priorslee, Shifnal, Shropshire   d: 1853 in Stourbridge
............+Elizabeth b: 1829
.................3 Mary Prou(w)dler   b: 1851 d: 1901
.... 2 Mary Proudler   b: 1828 in Born 17 Aug 1828 Priorslee baptisms
.... 2 Martha Proudler b: March 20, 1831 in Donnington Wood
............+Joseph Baker   b: 1828 m: September 1854 in Dudley Occupation: General labourer
.................3   John Proudler-Baker   b: 1862
.................3   Thomas Proudler-Baker   b: 1850
.... 2 John Proudler   b: 1833 d: 1834
.... 2 John Proudler   b: May 15, 1836 in Commonside, Kingswinford   d: July 2, 1902 in Pensnett
............+Mary Bunn b: 1838 m: 1857 in Dudley   d: January 5, 1875 in Pensnett
.... 3 Joseph Proudler   b: 1858 d: July 2, 1869 in Pensnett
.... 3 Elizabeth Proudler b: 1860
.... +? m: December 1884 in Hartlepool
.... 3 Mary Proudler b: 1863 in Kingswinford
.... +Henry Green m: September 1896 in Hartlepool
.... 3 John Proudler b: 1865 d: 1912
.... +Laura Kate b: 1875 m: June 1892 in Christchurch d: 1935 in Swindon
.... 4 Hedley Augustus Kenneth Proudler   b: 1895 in Shaftesbury   d: 1970
.... 4 Aubrey Sidney Proudler b: 1898 in Crickhowell   d: 1973
...............................+Doris Margaret Cowley b: 1906 m: June 1936 in Swindon, Wilts d: 1972
...............................5   David A. Proudler b: 1937 in Swindon
.... +June Warry m: September 1962 in Swindon, Wilts
...............................,,,,,, 6 Karla Louise Proudler   b: 1966 in Swindon
.... +John C. Durston m: September 1991 in Abingdon
.................3 Arthur Proudler b: 1868 in Stourbridge d: 1942 in Hartlepool
......................+Elizabeth Skelton b: 1870 m: June 1893 in Hartlepool d: 1958 in Hartlepool
.... 4 Elsie Anna Proudler   b: 1894 in Hartlepool d: 1894 in Hartlepool
.... 4 Arthur Godfrey Proudler b: 1897 in Hartlepool d: 1980
...............................+Ethel Bate b: 1895 m: September 1929 in Carlisle d: 1971
.....................................5 Stillborn   b: 1933 d: 1933
.....................................5   David G. Proudler b: 1935
.... +Elizabeth M. Henderson m: March 1962 in Wensleydale
.... 6 Christopher D. Proudler b: 1964 in Claro
.... 6 Ian William Proudler b: 1966 in Carlisle
....+Julie Noble m: May 1995 in Bridlington
.... 6 Timothy John Proudler b: 1967
.....................................5 Christine M. Proudler   b: 1939
.... +Ernest Veitch m: June 1961 in W. Hartlepool
.....................................5 Kathleen E. Proudler   b: 1939
.... +Martin Hope m: March 1962 in W. Hartlepool
.... 4 Millicent Proudler b: 1901
.............................+Howard Littlefair m: September 1925 in Hartlepool
.... 4 Ethel Maud Proudler   b: 1906 in Hartlepool
.... William Atkinson m: December 1928 in Hartlepool
.................3 Joseph Proudler   b: 1871 d: 1917
.... Emily Mary Furber   b: 1863 m: March 1893 in Stourbridge   d: 1939
.... 4 Winifred Alice Proudler b: 1894 in Stourbridge
...........................+John O'Leary   m: June 1923 in Stourbridge
.... 4 Frederick Charles Proudler   b: 1895   d: 1965
....+Florence Lavinia Venmore   b: 1896 in Spen Valley m: September 1920 in Dudley d: 1970
.... 5 Doris M. Proudler b: 1924
. ... +Percy H. Swallow m: June 1952 in Spen Valley
....,, 3   Sarah Proudler b: 1875
....,, +Enoch Raybould m: June 1897 in Stourbridge
.... 4 Ethel Raybould
.... 4 Polly Raybould
.... 4 Lily Raybould
.... 4 John Raybould
.... 4 Alan Raybould
.... 4 Ted Raybould
.... 4 Joe Raybould
.... *2nd Wife of John Proudler:
............+Catherine Clarke b: 1843 in Stafford m: 1876 d: 1916

.................3 Lydia Proudler b: 1877 d: 1918
.... +Leonard Thompson m: June 1907 in Dudley
.... 4 Lily Thompson
.... 4 Lee Thompson
.... 4 Harry Thompson
.... 4 Florence Thompson
.... 4 Cyril Thompson
.................3 Thomas Proudler   b: 1878 in Pensnett d: 1965 in Stourbridge
.... +Charlotte Clee b: 1877 m: December 24, 1898 in Pensnett d: 1957
.... 4 Wilfred Proudler b: August 6, 1900 in Pensnett, Kingswinford d: June 4, 1978
.................................+Ruth Peakman b: 1904 m: June 1923 in Stourbridge d: 1965
....5 Joan Proudler b: October 30, 1925
.... +Joe Banks
....*2nd Husband of Joan Proudler:
....+Reg Mallen m: December 1948 in Rowley Regis
.... 6 Gail Mallen b: Abt. 1948
....+Neil Bennett
....7 Philip Neil Bennett
....7 Kerrie Louise Bennett
.... *2nd Husband of Gail Mallen:
.... +Howard Clewes
.... 6 Patrick Mallen b: Abt. 1950
....+Dawn
.... 7 Ryan James Mallen
....5 Wilfred John Proudler (Jack)   b: July 4, 1928 in Kingswinford d: November 12, 1985
.... +Pam Guest m: November 14, 1953 in Rowley Regis
.... 6 Graeme John Proudler b: 1954
.... 6 Ian Keith Proudler b: 1956
.... 6 Trevor Lee Proudler b: 1960
....+Jayne E. Darby m: 1985 in Dudley
....7 Dean Lee Proudler b: 1987 in Stourbridge
....7 Caroline Louise Proudler b: 1989 in Stourbridge
....7 Heather Jean Proudler   b: 1993 in Stourbridge
.... 6 Valerie Kay Proudler b: 1965
.... +Adam V Chambers m: 1991 in Dudley
....5 Arthur Proudler b: October 3, 1929 in Kingswinford d: October 13, 2000 in Liverpool
....+Brenda Rea m: December 1956 in Dudley
.... 6 Alison Fay Proudler b: February 10, 1958
....+Phillip Green   m: June 1979 in Bootle
.... 6 Neil Fraser Proudler b: March 9, 1962
.... +Annastasia Coufopoulos b: August 10, 1965 m: June 20, 1987 in Sefton South
....7 Helen Ruth Proudler b: December 12, 1987 in Ormskirk Hospital
....7 Alexander Neil Proudler b: July 21, 1997 in Ormskirk Hospital
....5 Margarget Mary Proudler b: March 11, 1935 in Kingswinford
.... +Robin Lee m: September 1964 in Rowley Regis
.... 6 Julia Lee
.... +Nigel Fletcher
....7 Amelia Lee Fletcher
....7 Cameron Lee Fletcher
.... 6 Stephen Lee
.... +Maria
....7 Lucy Lee
....5 Sheila Proudler b: February 15, 1941
.... +Mick Writtle m: June 1964 in Rowley Regis
.... 6 Stuart Writtle
....+Joanne
....7 ABoy Writtle   b: September 2000
.... 6 Mark Writtle
.... 6 Matthew Writtle
.... 4 Arthur Proudler b: 1902 in Pensnett, Stourbridge   d: 1982 in Stourbridge
.................................+Lizzy Trevis b: 1904 m: June 1924 in Stourbridge d: 1972 in Stourbridge
....5 Doris I. Proudler b: 1924
.... +Andy Anderson m: December 1943 in Rowley Regis
.... 6 Linda Anderson
....5 Beryl Proudler b: 1935
.... +Frank Sullivan m: September 1953 in Rowley Regis
.... 6 Paul Sullivan   b: August 1963 in Rowley Regis, Staffordshire
.... 6 Maxine E. Sullivan b: Unknown
.................3 Ernest Proudlerb: 1882 in Stourbridge d: October 12, 1917 in Belgium
.... +Rebecca Marson b: Abt. 1890 m: June 1911 in Stourbridge

.... 4 Rebecca Proudler   b: 1912 d: June 1912 in Stourbridge
.... 4 Lynda Proudlerb: 1913 d: 1932
.... 4 Annie Proudler b: 1915 d: 1931
.... 2 Sarah Proudler b: March 28, 1839 in Kingswinford
............+William Flavill m: December 1857 in Dudley
.... 2 Thomas Proudler b: 1841 in Kingswinford d: 1899 in Pensnett
..........+Sobieska Bunn b: 1842 m: April 27, 1862 in Dudley St Thomas   d: 1924 in Stourbridge
.................3   Sarah Ann Proudler b: 1863 d: 1895 in Stourbridge
.................3   Agnes Proudler   b: 1864 d: 1942
.................3   **Albert Proudler** b: April 23, 1867 in Commonside, Pensnett   d: 1904 in Pensnett
.... +Ann Emmalaine (Emily) Baker   b: 1866 m: December 24, 1893 in St James, Dudley d: 1940 in Hendon, north
London
.... 4 Agnes Eveline Proudler (Lena)   b: 1895 in Stourbridge   Deceased
.... +Tom Harris m: September 1917 in St George Hanover Square, London
..................................5 John Harris   b: Unknown
..................................5 Marjorie (Joan) Harris b: February 1920 in Willesden
.... +Anthony J. R. Rowe m: May 1948 in Hendon, N. London
.... 6 David A. Rowe b: May 1951 in Willesden
.... 4 Francis Albert Proudler b: May 22, 1897 in Stourbridge d: 1955 in Canada
...............................+Ada Elida Kalaputas b: January 3, 1905 m: 1923 in Edmonton Canada d: December 10, 1999
.....................................5 Donald Ivan Proudler b: November 20, 1924   d: May 22, 1998
....+Barbara Thomas b: December 1, 1932 m: May 2, 1959
....6 Steven Robert Proudler   b: November 8, 1953
....+Barbara Barry b: August 2, 1953
....7 Andrew Blair (Drew) Proudler   b: July 21, 1979
....7 Jennifer Lynn Proudler b: September 1, 1982
.... 6 David Charles Proudler b: November 6, 1963 d: October 18, 1984
.....................................5 Dorothy May Proudler   b: May 21, 1927
.... 4Thomas Ivan Proudler b: 1899 in 11 Jan.Stourbridge d: April 13, 1917 in France
.... 4 Dorothy May Cordelia Proudler b: May 7, 1901 d: Deceased
...........................+Frank Fama m: December 1924 in Willesden, Middlesex
.................................5 Ron Fama b: May 11, 1926
.... +Noel Edith Gregory b: December 15, 1933   m: January 17, 1959
.... 6 Stephen Gregory Fama b: February 16, 1963
.... 6 Clare Marie Fama b: October 15, 1964
.................................+Anthony William Pitcher b: January 16, 1961
.................................7 Sarah Louise Pitcher b: February 2, 1995
.................................7 Timothy Josiah Pitcher b: September 5, 1996
.................................7 Kate Elizabeth Pitcher b: November 30, 1998
.................................5 Stella Carmelita Fama b: May 8, 1928   d: February 3, 1995
.... +Ronald Arthur Blackwell
.... 6 Stephen Blackwell b: 1964
.... 6 Leslie Blackwell   b: 1965
....5 Terence Joseph Fama   b: January 17, 1931
.................................5 John Louis Fama b: May 17, 1933
...................3 Jane Proudler b: 1869
.... +Mr Careless m: June 1913 in Stourbridge
...................3 Phoebe Proudler b: October 6, 1871 in Tansey Green, Pensnett
.... +Jeavon Greenway b: 1871 m: March 17, 1895 in Dudley
....   4 Frederick Proudler b: December 24, 1890 in Tansey Green, Pensnett d: 1960 in Died of a heart attack.
..............................+Annie MAY Timmins   b: December 3, 1888 m: December 1912 in Stourbridge d: 1978
....5 Edna May Proudlerb: May 4, 1913 in Kingswinford d. December 17, 1994 in USA
.... + Walter Dunning Powell b: May 10, 1920 m: December 1940 in Aldershot
.... 6 Walter Dunning Powell b: May 26, 1942 in Downham (Greater London), UK
...................................+Patricia Ann Alessie b: Abt. 1942 in Milford, Connecticut m: Abt. 1963
...................................7 Christopher Dunning Powell b: September 2, 1969
.... +Suzanne Riley
.... 8 Riley Dunning Powell   b: 2000
.... 8 Tanner Joseph Powell   b: December 2002
...................................7 Theodore Timothy Powell   b: September 4, 1971
.... +Lauri Van Name
.... 8 Olivia Laura Powellb: April 5, 2008 in Yale Hospital
...................................*2nd Husband of Edna May Proudler:
.... +Edmund Newcomb m: Abt. 1970
...................................5 Mary Evelyn Proudler b: February 26, 1915 in Kingswinford d: October 31, 1973
.... +Vic Goode b: July 30, 1913 m: June 1937 in Burton on Trent, Staffs d: October 2007
.... 6 Gillian Goode b: 1940 in Burton on Trent
...................................+George F. Cobley m: 1963 in Burton on Trent, Staffs
...................................7 Paul A. Cobley b: 1963
...................................7 Karen Cobley b: 1965

.... 6 John F Goode b: 1942 in Albany, USA
....+Anne m: 1969 in Albany, USA   d: 2003 in USA
....7 Gillian Goode b: Unknown
.... 8 Two girls ?b: Unknown
....7 Joanna Goode b: Unknown
.... 6 David Goode b: 1945
....7 Janet Goode b: Unknown
....7 Gillian Goode b: Unknown
.... 6 Janet Goode b: 1948 in Swadlincote
....+? Robey
.....................................5   Walter Frederick Proudler b: October 7, 1918 in Kingswinford   d: 1921
.....................................5   Frederick IVAN Proudler b: December 14, 1921 in Kingswinford
.... +Nora Chance   b: April 12, 1926 : March 1947 in Rowley Regis
.... 6 Frederick MARTIN Proudler   b: 1950 in Wall Heath, near Kingswinford
.....................................+Helena Howse b: 1952 in Wordsley, Stourbridge   m: March 1975 in Dudley
.....................................7 Joanne Proudler b: 1979
.....................................7 Elizabeth Proudler b: 1982
.... 6 Patrick I. Proudler b: 1953
.....................................+Evelyn Sargent m: December 1972 in Dudley
.....................................7 Lee Patrick Proudler b: 1973
.... +Debbie A. Kendrick m: 2001 in Torbay
.... 8 Lewis Samuel Proudler b: 2002 in Dudley
.... 8 Ellis Ian Proudler   b: 2004 in Dudley
.....................................7 Brian Proudler b: 1979
.....................................7 James Richard Proudler b: 1983
....+Gemma
.... 8 Lennon Proudler   b: Abt. 2005
.....................................5 Rhoda Annie Proudler   b: March 9, 1924 d: February 4, 1984
.... +Bill Carr m: June 1949 in Rowley Regis d: September 26, 1992 in Trinidad
.... 6 Anne Carr b: Abt. 1950
.....................................+Mr Thomas
.....................................7 [1] Sean Mitchell   b: Abt. 1975
.... +[2] ?
.... 8 [3] 1 dau ?
.... 8 [4] 2 dau ?
.....................................7 [5] Rachel Mitchell b: Abt. 1978
.... 8 [6] A son Mitchell
.... *2nd Husband of Anne Carr:
.... +Mr Mitchell
.... 7 [1] Sean Mitchell b: Abt. 1975
.... +[2] ?
.... 8 [3] 1 dau ?
.... 8 [4] 2 dau ?
.....................................7 [5] Rachel Mitchell b: Abt. 1978
.... 8 [6] A son Mitchell
.... 6 Billy Carr b: October 22, 1952 in Port of Spain, Trinidad
.....................................+Carol-Lyn May Johnson b: May 27, 1958 in Port of Spain, Trinidad m: November 26, 1977 in
Diego Martin, Trinidad
.....................................7 William Bowman Carr b: February 23, 1979 in Diego Martin, Trinidad
.... +?
.... 8? Carr
.....................................7 Trisha-Leigh Carr b: September 23, 1981 in Diego Martin, Trinidad
.... +?
.... 8 1 child ?
.... 8 2 child ?
.... 8 3 child ?
.... 6 John Carr b: 1956
.....................................+?
.... 7 Phil Carr b: 1989
.....................................7 Roseanna Carr b: 1990
.....................................7 Peter Carr b: 1992
.... 6 Jane Carr b: Abt. 1958
.....................................+Mr Lamkin
.....................................7 Nadine Lamkin b: Abt. 1984
.....................................7 Kristy Lamkin b: 1986
.....................................7 Ron Lamkin   b: 1988
.... *2nd Husband of Jane Carr:
.... +Greg Mackenzie
.... 6 Rachel Carrr   b: Unknown

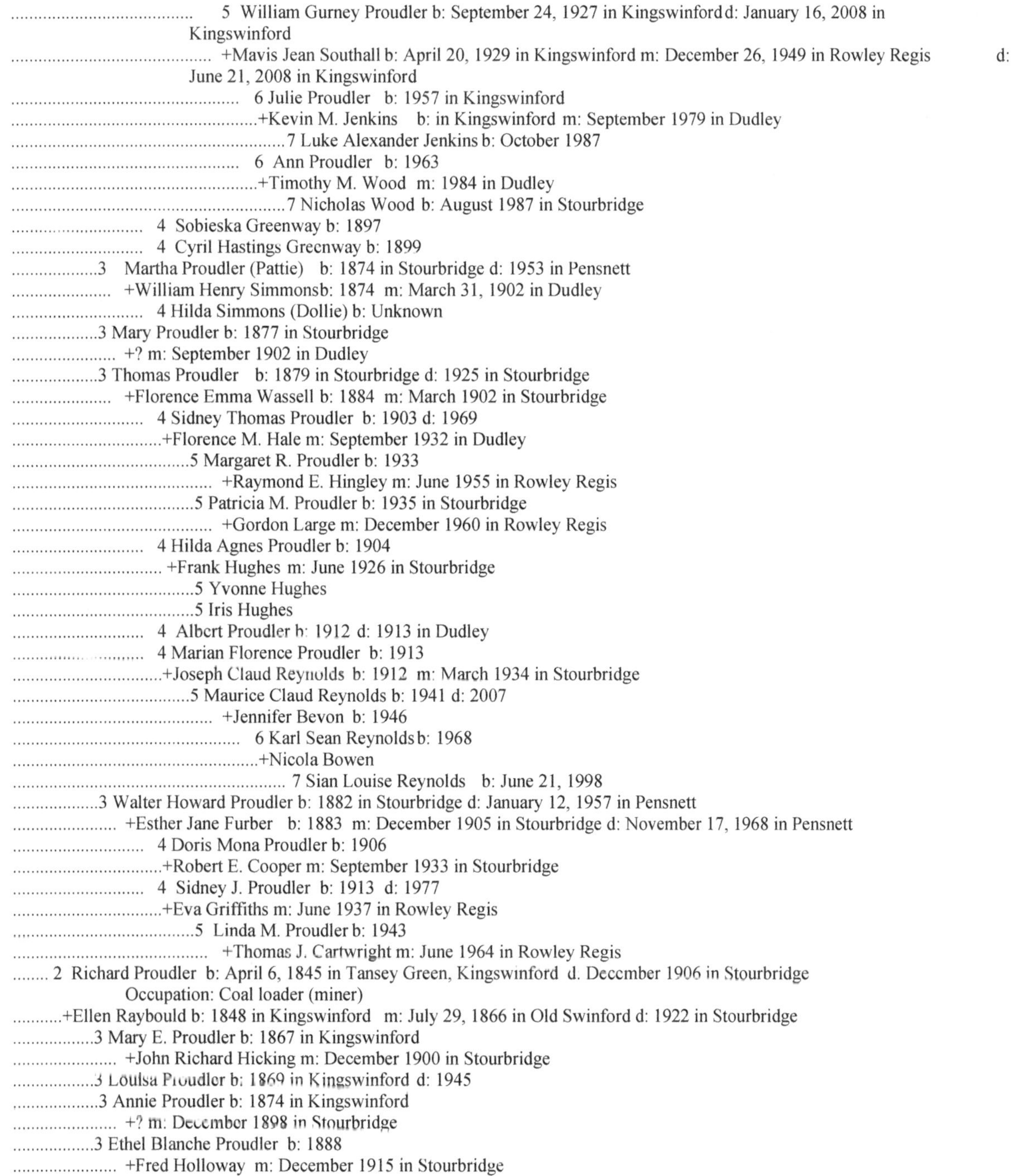

```
.........................................    5  William Gurney Proudler b: September 24, 1927 in Kingswinford d: January 16, 2008 in
                                          Kingswinford
.............................................    +Mavis Jean Southall b: April 20, 1929 in Kingswinford m: December 26, 1949 in Rowley Regis        d:
                                          June 21, 2008 in Kingswinford
...........................................    6  Julie Proudler   b: 1957 in Kingswinford
......................................+Kevin M. Jenkins   b: in Kingswinford m: September 1979 in Dudley
.....................................7 Luke Alexander Jenkins b: October 1987
...........................................    6  Ann Proudler   b: 1963
..................................+Timothy M. Wood  m: 1984 in Dudley
.....................................7 Nicholas Wood b: August 1987 in Stourbridge
............................    4  Sobieska Greenway b: 1897
............................    4  Cyril Hastings Greenway b: 1899
...............3   Martha Proudler (Pattie)   b: 1874 in Stourbridge d: 1953 in Pensnett
...................   +William Henry Simmons b: 1874  m: March 31, 1902 in Dudley
...............................    4  Hilda Simmons (Dollie) b: Unknown
...............3 Mary Proudler b: 1877 in Stourbridge
...................   +? m: September 1902 in Dudley
...............3 Thomas Proudler   b: 1879 in Stourbridge d: 1925 in Stourbridge
...................   +Florence Emma Wassell b: 1884  m: March 1902 in Stourbridge
...........................    4 Sidney Thomas Proudler  b: 1903 d: 1969
.............................+Florence M. Hale m: September 1932 in Dudley
.............................5 Margaret R. Proudler b: 1933
.....................................    +Raymond E. Hingley m: June 1955 in Rowley Regis
.............................5 Patricia M. Proudler b: 1935 in Stourbridge
...........................    +Gordon Large m: December 1960 in Rowley Regis
...........................    4  Hilda Agnes Proudler b: 1904
............................. +Frank Hughes m: June 1926 in Stourbridge
...............................5 Yvonne Hughes
...............................5 Iris Hughes
...........................    4  Albert Proudler b: 1912 d: 1913 in Dudley
...........................    4  Marian Florence Proudler  b: 1913
.........................+Joseph Claud Reynolds b: 1912  m: March 1934 in Stourbridge
.........................5 Maurice Claud Reynolds b: 1941 d: 2007
..............................    +Jennifer Bevon  b: 1946
.......................................    6 Karl Sean Reynolds b: 1968
......................................+Nicola Bowen
.............................................    7 Sian Louise Reynolds   b: June 21, 1998
...............3 Walter Howard Proudler b: 1882 in Stourbridge d: January 12, 1957 in Pensnett
...................   +Esther Jane Furber   b: 1883  m: December 1905 in Stourbridge d: November 17, 1968 in Pensnett
...................    4  Doris Mona Proudler b: 1906
.........................+Robert E. Cooper m: September 1933 in Stourbridge
...................    4  Sidney J. Proudler  b: 1913  d: 1977
.........................+Eva Griffiths m: June 1937 in Rowley Regis
...........................5  Linda M. Proudler b: 1943
..............................    +Thomas J. Cartwright m: June 1964 in Rowley Regis
........ 2  Richard Proudler  b: April 6, 1845 in Tansey Green, Kingswinford  d: December 1906 in Stourbridge
                Occupation: Coal loader (miner)
..........+Ellen Raybould b: 1848 in Kingswinford  m: July 29, 1866 in Old Swinford d: 1922 in Stourbridge
...............3 Mary E. Proudler b: 1867 in Kingswinford
...................   +John Richard Hicking m: December 1900 in Stourbridge
...............3 Louisa Proudler b: 1869 in Kingswinford d: 1945
...............3 Annie Proudler b: 1874 in Kingswinford
...................   +? m: December 1898 in Stourbridge
...............3 Ethel Blanche Proudler  b: 1888
...................   +Fred Holloway  m: December 1915 in Stourbridge
```

John Proudler 1800-1860 - son of Joseph

Joseph's son JOHN[9] PROUDLER *(JOSEPH[8], PETER[7] PROUDLEY, JOHN[6], RICHARD[5], THOMAS[4], WILLIAM[3], PERSEVILE[2], ?[1])* was born 1800 in Shifnal. He moved away from Shropshire roughly south-easterly to the West Midlands where there would have been many more work opportunities and settled in the Shut End district of Pensnett. Pensnett, at this time, would have looked very different from how it does today. The hamlet where the Proudlers settled - off Tansey Green Road/Commonside - was right next to a coal mine: the Shut End Coal Pit. Indeed, part of a local chapel suffered with subsidence from the underground mining. According to the Baptismal Register 1845-87 for the Shut End Primitive Methodist Chapel, the chapel was run by the Rev Henry Higginson, "commonly known as the 'Roving Ranter'". So the Proudlers settled in this area, living in small terraced workers cottages, usually in overcrowded conditions. They would have attended the local Chapel for baptisms and such events but burials took place at the nearby church of St Marks - which is located just at the end of Commonside. Today St Marks is an oasis of calm tucked inside a busy urban sprawl. John had married in Shropshire, before they left that county, to Elizabeth FORGHAM on May 9, 1825 in Wellington. He was employed as a labourer and they lived at Tansey Green in Pensnett. She was born 1804, and died October 22, 1886 in Pensnett. They are both buried at St Mark's Church and we have found their grave which, to date, is the earliest Proudler grave located. After John's death, on the 1881 census, Elizabeth can be found living with her son John.

Graves (right) of both John and Elizabeth. Left-hand grave is the oldest known surviving PROUDLER gravestone: St Mark's Church, Pensnett, West Midlands.   Directions to find grave: through the entrance gate and follow the left path (passing the church on your right), grave located to your left down the path a little way.

Monumental Inscription:

In Affectionate Remembrance of: JOHN PROUDLER, (late of Tansey Green)Who departed this life in 1860 (age 60 years) "An honest man, Industrious, Free from Strife, Harmless, he pass'd the Vale of Human Life, The Best of Husbands, Father and of Friends, Beloved by all, till here his existence ends, And his mortal path conspires the dust, That his spirit may live, where joys await the just, Also ELIZABETH PROUDLER, wife of the above, Who died October 22nd, 1886, age 83 years. Her end was peace.

The grave immediately to the right of theirs, contains their son John b. 1832, his wife and their son Joseph who died aged 10.
The right-hand grave says the following:

*in affectionate remembrance of Joseph, son of John and Mary PROUDLER of Tansey Green
Who died July 2nd, 1869, aged 10 years and 9 months.
Also Mary, wife of John PROUDLER, who died January 5th 1875 aged 37 years and 9 months
Farewell my partner dear farewell, A long farewell to thee
And you my children dear, farewell, No more my face you'll see
Also John, husband of the above, Who died July 21st 1902, aged 66 years.
Day by day yet more we miss him, None but aching heart can tell
Earth has lost him, heaven has gained him, Jesus hath done all things well.*

Thomas Proudler 1841-99 - son of John

A short distance away from John and Elizabeth's grave, is that of their son Thomas 1841-99 and his family.
Thank you to Pam PROUDLER for restoring this grave

*In Loving Memory of Sarah Ann
The beloved daughter of Thomas and Sobieska PROUDLER Tansey Green, Pensnett, who died 1st April 1895, age 32 years.
She is gone, but not forgotten, Never will her memory fade, Fondest thoughts will ever linger, Round the place where she is laid.
Also of the above named Thomas PROUDLER who died 5th Feb 1899 Aged 56 year, Thy will be done. Also of Albert eldest son of the above, Who passed away 24th January 1904, In his 36th year. In the midst of life we are in death. Also of Sobieska The beloved wife of Thomas PROUDLER Of Tansey Green Who passed away 10th May 1924, Aged 82 years, The rest shall have peace.*

CHILDREN OF THOMAS AND SOBIESKA

Thomas (above) 1841-99 was married to Sobieska Bunn. Sobieska's sister (Mary) had married Thomas's brother John; so two Bunn sisters married two Proudler brothers.

Walter Howard Proudler 1882-1957	Phoebe Proudler (right) b. 1871	Albert Proudler (bow tie) 1867-1904

Descendants of Thomas and Sobieska's children are spread far and wide, including: Walter's descendants currently reside in Pensnett, descendants of Phoebe are in America today and descendants of Albert are in Canada and New Zealand.

Phoebe Proudler b. 1871 (daughter of Thomas and Sobieska)

Phoebe has an illegitimate child, Frederick (1890-1960), who can be seen on the picture on the next page - The Shut End Prize Brass Band in 1902. Frederick is there as a young 12 year old boy on the front row. His occupation was blacksmith. Phoebe was married in 1895 to a Jeavon Greenway and had two further children with him. Son Frederick married Annie May Timmins in 1912 and had six children:

Edna May 1913-94	Gurney 1927-2008	Rhoda 1924-84

Tom PROUDLER (1878-1965) <u>sat behind the base drum...</u>

.. and the boy sitting on the front row, right, is believed to be **<u>Frederick PROUDLER (1890-1960)</u>**[5]**.** There may well be more PROUDLERs in this picture, but it was difficult for family members to identify them. Possibly there is also **<u>Thomas PROUDLER (1879-1925)</u>** on the back row second from right. There are at least four related families in this picture: PROUDLERS, GREENWAYS, SIMMONS and BARNSLEY. Date of the above picture has been estimated to be about 1902 – from the age of Frederick (boy) in front row (1890-1960). The boy sitting to the left of the base drum is **<u>Joe BARNSLEY, aged 12 yrs</u>**, holding a clarinet. His brother is 3rd from the right on the back row. Joe's address was Glendale, Commonside, Pensnett, PROUDLERs were also living at Commonside at this time. The SIMMONS family were related to the PROUDLERs, i.e. marriage of Martha PROUDLER to William Henry SIMMONS born 1877.

EDNA May Proudler 1913-94

married (1) WALTER DUNNING POWELL December 1940 in Aldershot, son of WALTER POWELL and ALBERTA O'CONNOR. He was born May 10, 1920. She married (2) EDMUND NEWCOMB Abt. 1970.

---

[5] Death Certificate records Frederick's occupation as Blacksmith.

Emigrated to America on 28 June 1939, her descendants are still there today. Picture (above, before Band photo) was taken on the beach at Devon about 1938-9. She sailed from Hull to Montreal Canada on the "Bassano", captain A.H. Best. Ellerman's Wilson Shipping Line. Cabin class.   Occupation: Nanny pre-war. Edna's son "Dunny", was 20 blocks away from the World Trade Centre on September 11th, 2001. He is an architect and was on site for an early morning conference with site engineers when the first aircraft flew low overhead. He took the following picture as the terrorist attack began ...

On arrival in Canada, Edna initially worked as a governess. She also met her future husband there. Walter Dunning POWELL (3rd) was with the Canadian Army Black Watch – he had also been stationed at Aldershot, England and this seems to be where the couple marry – December quarter 1940.

Thanks to the son of Edna May PROUDLER – Walter Dunning POWELL (IV) for information on this line and the above picture.

Frederick Ivan Proudler b.1921 (son of Frederick 1890-1960)

PROUDLER – CHANCE 1947

On Saturday at St Mary's Church, Kingswinford, Miss Nora CHANCE, third daughter of Mr and Mrs W. CHANCE, 65 Blaze Park, Wullheath was married to Mr Ivan PROUDLER, second son of Mr and Mrs F. PROUDLER, 18 Summer Street, Kingswinford. The bride, who was given in marriage by her father, wore a gown of white lace over heavy silk, full-length veil and head-dress of orange blossoms. She carried a bouquet of red carnations and trailing fern. The bridesmaid, Miss R. PROUDLER (sister of the bridegroom) was attired in a full-length dress of blue figured satin, with feathered head-dress and muff to match. The best man was Mr Ralph CHANCE (eldest brother of the bride). The bridegroom's gift to the bride was a gold locket and chain, and his gift to the bridesmaid, a silver charm bracelet. The bride's gift to the bridegroom was a fountain pen. The service was conducted by the Rev.J.F. PARKER (vicar) and the organist (Mr HAMBREY) played appropriate music. The reception was held in the Church Hall, Kingswinford, some 40 guests being present. The toast of "Bride and Bridegroom" was proposed by her father. After the reception, music for dancing was played by Malcolm COLLINS and his band. The bride and groom were the recipients of monetary gifts and useful presents. Lucky horse-shoes were presented to the bride by Masters Allan CHANCE, John BUTLER and little Linda GREENAWAY.

Rhoda Annie Proudler 1924-84

Rhoda Annie, like her older sister Edna, also emigrated from England, but Rhoda went to Trinidad where she married Bill CARR (d. 1992) in 1949 and had five children. Bill CARR's occupation was Head of Red Cross for Trinidad and Tobago. It is believed that Ann CARR, one of their daughters lives in Trinidad. A son William (Billy) born 1952 moved to England, he has two children. Another son James died aged only two following unsuccessful surgery on his intestines. Another son John born circa 1958 has three children. Another daughter, Jane born circa 1960 is believed to be in Nova Scotia, Canada. Rhoda died of colon cancer at age 60, in 1984. Following is the newspaper announcement of her engagement:

> *Engagement: MR W.B. CARR AND MISS R.A. PROUDLER*
> *This engagement is announced between William, the only son of*
> *Mr and Mrs W. B. CARR, Caripito, Venezuela, S.A. and Rhoda,*
> *youngest daughter of Mr and Mrs F. PROUDLER, 18 Summer Street,*
> *Kingswinford.*

Rhoda was a bridesmaid at brother Ivan's wedding in 1947. She visited her sister Edna's family in 1949 when they were leaving England, then again in 1953 and 1954 for the Queen's tour of the Empire. She emigrated to Trinidad in the late 1940s.

William "Gurney" PROUDLER 1927-2008

Married to Mavis (1929-2008) and both died within months of each other. We spoke on the phone to Mavis in the early days of trying to put this family history together and they were both extremely helpful with information that allowed us to begin piecing together the West Midlands branch of the family. He served in the navy during WWII.

Albert Proudler 1867-1904- (son of Thomas and Sobieska)

Albert, unfortunately, died young. It is believed that he had chest problems probably caused by working in the coal mines and died soon after the photograph on the following page was taken. His wife, Emily, was left with four children and no means of support; so she put the two sons into Barnado's Homes and kept her two daughters. Both sons were subsequently, and separately, sent to Canada to work on farms. Fortunately they were placed on adjoining farms in their new home. Then, at the outbreak of World War I, Thomas enlisted whilst Albert joined up when he was drafted. Only Albert survived.

Children of ALBERT PROUDLER and EMILY BAKER are:
  i.   AGNES EVELINE PROUDLER (LENA), b. 1895, Stourbridge; d. Deceased.
  ii. FRANCIS ALBERT PROUDLER, b. May 22, 1897, Stourbridge; d. 1955, Canada.
  iii. THOMAS IVAN PROUDLER, b. 1899, 11 Jan. Stourbridge; d. April 13, 1917, France.

Left to right: Ann Emmaline(Emily) PROUDLER holding baby Dorothy in her lap, Lena PROUDLER, Albert PROUDLER. Sitting on his lap Thomas Ivan PROUDLER and, sitting on the floor, Francis Albert PROUDLER (called Albert). Picture taken about 1902, Pensnett/Stourbridge.

Right - Thomas Ivan PROUDLER (little boy sitting on his father's lap in previous photo) who died aged only 18 years. Thomas Ivan PROUDLER was sent by Barnardos to Canada at only 11 years of age to work on a farm. He later enlisted in WWI and was subsequently sent to France to fight and found himself near Vimy Ridge. We visited his grave (right) some years ago which is at the Bruay Communal Cemetery. We believe that his unit was charged with defending an area known as The Pimple – just off the Vimy Ridge area which was bitterly fought over the day after the battle ended. His gravestone is somewhat faded with time, but excellently maintained by the Commonwealth War Graves Commission.

The Barnardo Foundation sent 100,000 children to Commonwealth countries where labour was needed on farms. Thomas
Ivan PROUDLER was sent on SS Tunisian on 10 March 1910,
departed Liverpool arriving Halifax, Canada on 18th March 1910.
Age 11 years. Destination is listed as "To Toronto and
Peterborough Ont". This practice of sending unaccompanied
children and orphans overseas to work was outlawed in
subsequent years.

Thomas worked at Blackburn Farm (between Uxbridge and
Glen Major). He enlisted in WWI at Lindsay, but his 38th Btn
unit was based at Ottawa.

Brother, Albert, was sent to work on an adjoining farm for
Meredith Rowntree. Albert waited till the Draft to join up.
So both boys were situated close to each other. Thomas died of wounds at No. 22 Casualty Clearing
Station (Canadian Archives)

*Thanks to Linda Grandfield for finding out what happened to the boys in Canada. Linda is a descendant
of the boys' Aunt Frances Baker.*

The other children of Albert and Emily Proudler:-

Francis Albert Proudler and wife Ada Kalaputus
1897-1955   1905-99

Lena Proudler b.1895

Francis Albert PROUDLER 1897-1955 was also, separately, sent to
Canada as a Barnardo Boy, but he survived WWI. He sailed on
the ship The Dominion from Liverpool to Portland, Canada on
21 February 1907, aged 9. (He is listed as age 8). Arrival date 5th March 1907.

Lena is pictured above right with new husband Thomas Harris at marriage.

At the outbreak WWI Francis 'Albert' was conscripted to army service where it is believed he worked in the medical field. He survived the war, returned to Canada , married Ada in 1923 and had a daughter Dorothy (unmarried) and a son Donald (deceased).   Francis Albert PROUDLER's wife Ada, kept a wonderful record of the couple's adventures as they bought and settled land in Canada ....

This account of their arrival in Caroline, Alberta was written prior to 1984

The Albert PROUDLER Family in Canada

By Ada PROUDLER (1905-1999)

We moved to the Caroline district the first of November 1936 from Sylvan Lake with our two children, Donald and Dorothy. As it took more than one truck load to move, the horses were taken first. It was a long hard trip as it had been raining and the roads were almost impassable in spots. The truck slid off the road near Evergreen and the horses had to be unloaded to pull it back on the road. The team proceeded to Caroline under their own steam and made almost as good time as the truck. The furniture arrived with us on the next load, and we had better weather for this trip.
It was the first experience for the children in farm life and going to a country school. They attended the Wooler School and their first teacher was Grace WALDROFF.

Both Albert and I had been raised on the farm, so we knew what was ahead of us – hard work and not much money.   Albert was born in Glasgow, Scotland and came to Ontario as a child. He and his younger brother enlisted in the Army during the First World War. His brother lost his life in France. Albert was a steam engineer by trade and ran steam engines on the prairie for harvesting and land breaking. I was born in the district of Sylvan Lake and attended Melita and Kewsamo Schools. We were married in 1923 in Edmonton. Don was born in Minneapolis, Minnesota and Dorothy in Sulvan Lake.

The land we bought at Caroline was purchased from Mr and Mrs TRENHOLME and was the N.W.Q.9-36-6-5. This quarter section of land was homesteaded by Mr George PALMER. Our farming was done mainly by horses. The first tractor we bought was an old John Deere Waterloo, but it was heavy, slow and awkward and was not of much use except for breaking land and grinding grain. Later we purchased a Hart Parr tractor and grain separator which was used for threshing our own crops as well as the neighbours. Farming never really became mechanized for us until after the Second World War The roads were always a concern when a trip further than Caroline was made, as it usually always rained when we were away, and the task of returning home would become almost impossible. I remember one trip we made to Red Deer. It was a beautiful day when we left home, but the clouds came up from the west and, after a continuous rain, we were all night and part of the next day getting home. We usually alerted the neighbours before a trip so the chores would get done if we didn't return.

In 1953 we built a house in Caroline and moved from the farm to town because of Albert's ill health. He sold insurance and was Justice of the Peace until his passing in January 1955. I carried on the business until 1961 when I moved to Red Deer. I have since lived in different parts of Canada.

* * *

Albert is buried at a military plot in Red Deer, Alberta, Canada. Albert (above) was born 22 May 1897 but grave says 1898. His wife Ada is buried at a family burial plot.

Dorothy May Cordelia Proudler b. 1901

Wedding of Dorothy PROUDLER to Frank FAMA on 27 October 1924. (Dorothy was pictured previously in a group photo with her family - she was the baby being held by her mother in the picture dated about 1902).

Picture right - Man in the middle row with a boutonniere (button hole) would be the best man D. PEARS (presumably from the groom's side of the family). Front row: Groom Frank FAMA in the centre with bride Dorothy PROUDLER. To the right of the bride is her mother, Ann Emmaline (Emily) PROUDLER who also signs the marriage certificate as a witness and Frances Baker Clarke (bride's Aunt). Wedding took place at Our Lady of Willesden R.C. Church, London.

Martha Proudler 1874-1953 (daughter of Thomas and Sobieska)

Obituary Notice for Martha PROUDLER

Martha was the daughter of Thomas PROUDLER & Sobieska BUNN. Martha (used the name Pattie) and married William Henry SIMMONS on 31st March 1902. So the following Obituary Notice is hers.

> The death of Mrs Pattie SIMMONS occurred at her home, 25 Cooper's Bank, Pensnett on January 29th in her 79th year. The funeral took place at St Mark's Church, Pensnett, on Saturday. A number of relatives and friends attended the choral service, which was conducted by the Rev. L. U. SMITH. Mr MORRIS was organist and the choir was in attendance. The mourners were: Miss Hilda (Dollie) SIMMONS (daughter), Mr Walter PROUDLER and Mr Fred PROUDLER (brothers), Mrs Jane CARELESS and Phoebe GREENWAY (sisters), Mrs Tom HARRIS (niece), Mr Sidney PROUDLER, Mr Albert WIGGAN, Mr Tom HARRIS, Mr John BRADLEY and Mr William JOINSON (nephews). The bearers were Messrs Cyril GREENWAY, William STEVENS, Bob COOPER, Fred COLLEY, Gurney PROUDLER-nephews.

Thank you to Walter Dunning Powell IV for this Obituary

Thomas Proudler 1879-1925

(Not to be confused with the other Thomas Proudler of Pensnett 1878-1965)

Both Thomas Proudlers, of about same age, are thought to be depicted on the Shutt End Prize Band Photograph of 1902. The 1911 census distinguishes the two cousins:

> Thomas 1879-1925: Thomas, age 31, occupation painter, married to Florence, age 28, with children Sydney T. PROUDLER age 7 and Hilda A. Age 6. Address 13 Bradley St.

> Thomas 1878-1965: Thomas PROUDLER, age 32, occupation coal miner, with wife Charlotte, age 34, and two children Wilfred age 10 and Arthur age 9. (Wilfred is the father of the footballer Arthur PROUDLER).

Thomas 1879-1925 served in WWI. His Pensioner's Record Card has been obtained which states his address to be 13 Bradley Street. This address was recorded on 9 December 1915 at Birmingham where he was undertaking a Medical Examination. His occupation is "painter and decorator". Plus, we have personal correspondence from Maurice REYNOLDS (grandson), telling us he was a painter.

Thomas was awarded the Victory Medal, the British Medal and The Star following his service in France.

Right is a picture sent to us by Maurice REYNOLDS (now deceased) showing his mother Marion Florence PROUDLER standing by her father's (Thomas PROUDLER's) grave; date unknown but looks to have been taken 1930s/1940s. Location of grave not known, but may be also at St Mark's Pensnett.

Other information from his military records include:
height 5ft 5.5" tall, 132 lbs, chest measurement 36 inches, range of expansion 3.5 inches. Vaccinated: infancy. Enlisted Birmingham 9th Dec 1915.
Medical problems: seem to have Myalgia dating from 1900; rheumatic pains all over his body; legs are principally affected, cannot walk far. Rank: Private. Thomas PROUDLER, regiment number 277985 (labour?), there is a note (crossed through) saying "transferred to 48th Training Reserves".
There are further medical notes dated 1918, 1919 and 1920. It is known that he died in 1925.

Maurice Reynolds kindly provided information on this line of descent.

John Proudler 1836-1902 (son of John 1800-1860)

So, we've seen that John's brother Thomas 1841-1899 produces one line of Proudlers in Pensnett that spreads to America, Canada and New Zealand; now we can look at John's line of descent which will spread beyond Stourbridge in the West Midlands to Hartlepool, Swindon.

John was married to Mary Bunn 1838-75. He married her in 1857, then five years later his brother Thomas marries Sobieska Bunn (Mary's sister). But Mary dies in 1875 - probably in child birth as her youngest daughter Sarah is born at that time. Within a year, John has married for a second time to Catherine Clarke 1843-1916. When he dies, John is buried next to his first wife Mary.

Ernest Proudler 1882-1917

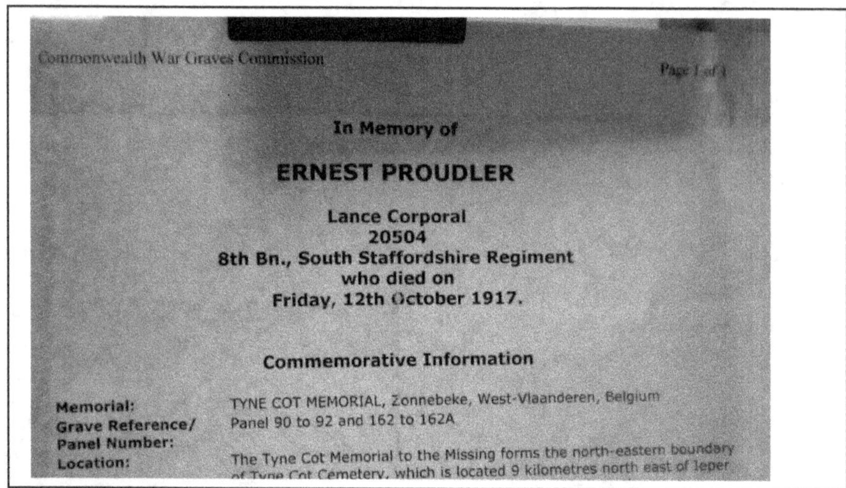

Ernest was the youngest child (son of John and Catherine). He married in 1911 and had three daughters - all died as infants. He enlisted for service in World War One but sadly was killed in action at Ypres in Belgium.

There is no grave for Ernest but a plaque at the Tyne Cot Memorial Site in Belgium to his memory. It is believed that he was killed at the First Battle of Paschendale. Ernest's Service Record shows him Killed in Action, Theatre of War France and Flanders. 8th Service Battalion details: Formed at Lichfield September 1914 – K2 to Wareham in 51st Battalion 17th Division then West Lulworth and Wool. June 1915 to Winchester area. 14th July 1915 landed at Boulogne. 23rd February 1918 disbanded; personnel to 2/6th and 8th Battalions and 7th Entrenching Battalion. Awarded the Victory and British Medals (F/101B9 1058)

Proudlers in Swindon and Hartlepool

The children of John b. 1836 and Mary Bunn are responsible for starting branches that move away from Pensnett.   It seems that the first to move in the direction of Hartlepool was their daughter Elizabeth who, though born in Pensnett, marries in Hartlepool and thereafter she is joined there by brother Arthur and sister Mary - who all settle in that area. John b. 1836 has a son also called John b.1865 who marries Kate and it is their two sons who make the move away from Pensnett to Swindon in Wiltshire.

HEDLEY AUGUSTUS KENNETH PROUDLER, b. 1895, Shaftesbury; d. 1970.
Nts: Unmarried, served in WWI.
Occupation: Railway clerk, worked at Swindon Railways: "A" Erecting Shop - there is a memorial plaque at the new (2000) Millennium Railway Museum in Swindon which commemorates the Great Western Railway which lists him- and those who went to War and returned. Hedley's war record states that he was with the Royal Naval Volunteer Reserve at Chatham, Royal Navy Dockyard. His "ship" is listed as

Pembroke – and from what we can gather, this is not an actual ship, but reference to an administrative home-based naval base/an accounting base. Date and period of engagement: 29 May 1916 – hostilities. Height: 5'-6.5" tall; chest (inches) 33.5"; Hair: brown; Eyes: blue; Complexion: Fair. Perhaps Hedley was lucky to survive, as 242 men died at the Pembroke naval establishment of Spanish Influenza in the period 1918 to 1921. His length of service was at least from 1916 to 1919 as his war service record states his conduct as being "very good" at 31.12.1916, then again 31.12.1917, then 31.12.1918 and lastly 31.7.1919. There is a reference to him receiving a "badge" on 29.5.1919. So, it looks like his service ended July 1919. There is reference to him having been paid War Gratuity, though the date is unclear.

AUBREY SIDNEY PROUDLER 1898-1973 is also resident in Swindon.

Thomas Proudler 1878-1965

(Not to be confused with the other Thomas Proudler of Pensnett 1879-1925) Thomas is depicted in The Shut End Prize Band Photo of 1902. He married Charlotte Clee in 1898 and had two sons Wilfred and Arthur.

Wilfred 1900-1978 - son of Thomas 1878-1965

Wilfred Proudler 1900-78

Arthur Proudler 1929-2000
(son of Wilfred)

Arthur (centre) and Jack Proudler (right) 1928-85
(brothers) taken about 1947-48

Arthur PROUDLER 1929-2000

Arthur PROUDLER was a Professional Footballer for Aston Villa, then later Crystal Palace. Later in life (in 1996) he, and his family, moved up to Liverpool where he became coach for Everton. Apart from football, he ran his own business before finally working at Ashworth Hospital as a nurse before retirement. At his funeral in 2000, many good friends and family attended. The eulogy was given by

Brian LABONE (ex-England and Everton Captain), also attended by Gordon WEST (Ex-England and Everton) and Alan WHITTLE, plus Stuart IMLAC (F.A. Cup medal).

Thomas Proudler 1797-1832

Thomas, son of Joseph and Martha Proudler - a labourer, never leaves Shropshire but branches of some of the largest lines of descent come from his children: From his son John 1829-1919 the branch of Proudlers in America descend, Derbyshire from his daughter Sarah b. 1824, but first, his son Thomas 1832-78 who begins the Yorkshire descent .....

Thomas Proudler 1832-78 *Descendants of Thomas Proudler*

1 Thomas Proudler b: 1832 in Donington Wood, Shropshire d: June 1878 in Sheffield
.. +Mary Tudor b: 1827 in St Georges, Shifnal m: September 1851 in Shifnal, Shropshire d: 1896 in Sheffield
   2 Mary Ann Proudler b: March 25, 1851 in Shifnal   d: January 14, 1924
...........+Charles Brown b: 1847 m: December 1872 in Shifnal, Shropshire d: March 9, 1929
.... 3Sarah J Brown b: April 10, 1876 in Sheffield d: September 30, 1915
..................3 Charles Leonard Brown b: November 18, 1880 in Sheffield d: January 13, 1882
.... 2 John Proudler b: 1853 d: 1934
...........+Emma b: 1852 in Thorpe, Lincoln m: December 1872 in Sheffield d: 1916 in Sheffield
................3Thomas Proudler b: 1873 in Sheffield d: 1876 in Sheffield
.... 2 Martha Proudler b: 1857 in Shifnal
...........+Frederick Allcock b: 1855 in Sheffield m: June 1880 in Sheffield
..................3 Maud Allcock b: 1881
................3 Harry Allcock b: 1885
................3 William A. Allcock b: 1887
...............3 Leonard Allcock b: 1889
................3 Mabel Allcock b: 1891
.... 2 Thomas Proudler b: 1859 in St Georges, Shropshire d: 1943
...........+Emily Shorthose b: 1858 in Sheffield m: December 1879 in Ecclesall d: 1933
................3Thomas Henry Proudler b: January 13, 1880 in Brightside, Sheffield d: 1968
.....................+Mary Ann Hall (aka Polly)   b: April 4, 1873 in Haverton Hill, Durham   m: December 1900 in Stockton   d: 1964
...........................4 Maurice Ashmore Proudler b: August 11, 1901 in Haverton Hill d: 1948
..............................+Winifred Mary Green b: 1898 m: June 1926 in Middlesbrough, Yorkshire d: 1990
..................................5 Francis Aubrey Proudler b: 1927 in London d: November 2003 in Enfield, London
.... 5 John Colin Proudler b: October 29, 1928 in Middlesbrough
...............................+Rita Darragh m: September 1955 in Middlesbrough, Yorkshire
.... 6 Geraldine Ann Proudler b: July 2, 1956 in Middlesbrough
.... +Graham P.K. Huntley m: 2000 in Kensington, London
.... 6 John Mark Proudler b: September 22, 1957 in Saltburn
.... +Penelope J. Bailey or Reynolds m: June 1990 in Westminster, London
.... 7 Edward Colin Proudler b: 1993 in Hillingdon
.... *2nd Wife of John Mark Proudler:
.....................................+Penelope J. Reynolds m: June 1990 in Westminster, London
.... 7 Alexandra Jane Proudler   b: 1991 in Westerminster, London
.... 6 Margaret Louise Proudler b: January 9, 1959 in Saltburn
.... 6 Johanna Marie Proudler b: August 11, 1960
.... +Brian O'Gorman
.... 7 Ben Gerard O'Gorman b: August 1988
.... 7 Tom Colin O'Gorman b: December 1989
.... 7 Polly Johanna O'Gorman b: April 1991
.... 7 Rory Brian O'Gorman b: May 1993
.... 6 Alexandra Carmel Proudler b: February 16, 1964 in Saltburn
.... +Nicholas Guyatt m: October 2005 in Huntingdon
.... 6 Frances Anne Proudler b: September 6, 1966 in Middlesbrough
.... +Blat
..................................5 Vincent Alan Proudler b: 1930 in Scotland
.... +Alexandra Sarah Douglas m: June 1959 in Middlesbrough, Yorkshire d: December 13, 1993 in Scotland
.... 6 Sarah Louise Proudler b: June 20, 1960 in Scotland
.... 6 Stephen Roger Proudler b: December 23, 1961 in Scotland
.... +?
.... 7 Sandy Proudler b: 1993
.... *2nd Wife of Stephen Roger Proudler:
.... +Dawn Ann Wilson
.... 7Callum Proudler b: 1995
.... 7 Ryan Proudler b: 1997
.... 6 Theresa Jane Proudler b: August 20, 1963 in Scotland

.... 6 Martin Douglas Proudler b: November 7, 1968 in Scotland
.... +Ms Fenimore m: 2000 in Middlesbrough
.... 7 Lewis Proudler b: Unknown
.... 7 Christopher Proudler b: Unknown
.... 6 Suzanne Helen Proudler b: February 19, 1974 in Scotland
.... 7 Ila ?b: Unknown
.....................................5 Stuart Anthony Proudler b: 1931
..................................+Rita Ryder m: March 1953 in Middlesbrough, Yorkshire d: 1997
...............................6 Gerard V Proudler b: 1956
.... +Hae-Young
.... 7 Jason Proudler b: August 18, 1988
.... 7 Catherine Proudler b: April 20, 1990
.... 7 Kevin Proudler b: February 11, 1992
.... 6 Kevin Sean Proudler b: 1957
.... 6 Susan Maria Proudler b: 1958 d: 1958 in Durham
.....................................5 Brian Gerard Proudler b: December 24, 1932 in Middlesbrough d: November 2000 in Middlesbrough
..................................+Jean Margaret Callaghan b: February 26, 1939 in Middlesbrough m: September 1957 in Middlesbrough,
.... 6 Lynn Margaret Proudler b: November 15, 1958 in Middlesbrough
.... +Martin C. Cook b: in Clevelandm: July 1985 in Cleveland
.... 6 Christine Anne Proudler b: December 25, 1960 in Newport Mon.
.... +Stephen Todd m: September 1981 in Cleveland
.... 6 Angela Patricia Proudler b: April 10, 1962
.... +Geoffrey H. Hughes m: September 1983 in Cleveland
.... 5 Sheila Mary Proudler b: 1935 in Scotland
.... +Donald MacFarlane m: June 1957 in Middlesbrough, Yorkshire d: November 17, 2007 in Scotland
.... 5 John Gordon Proudler b: 1936
.... +Ann Turley b: 1939 in Middlesbrough m: December 1962 in Cleveland
.... 6 Monica Ruth Proudler b: Abt. 1965
.... 6 John Dominic Proudler b: Abt. 1966 in Toronto, Canada
.... +Monica Santin
.... 7 Benjamin Joseph Proudler b: 1986
.....................................5 Michael Henry Proudler b: 1943
..................................+Jennifer Swalwell m: December 1967 in Middlesbrough, Yorkshire
.... 6 Robert Andrew Proudler b: November 4, 1969
..................................+Deborah Fender b: 1973 m: 1992 in Macclesfield
.....................................7 Samantha Jane Proudler b: 1991
.... *2nd Wife of Robert Andrew Proudler:
.....................................+Joane m: 2009
.... 6 Clare Marie Proudler b: April 7, 1971
.... +Andrew K. Stevenson m: October 1987 in Trafford, Cheshire
.... 7 Amy Catherine Stevenson b: April 1988 in Macclesfield
.... 7 Sarah Marie Stevenson b: November 1989 in Manchester
.... 7 Olivia Folasade R Stevenson b: February 2001 in Lancaster
.... 6 Jacqueline Ann Proudler b: November 9, 1973
.... +Neil L. Brown m: 1995 in Southampton
.....................................7 Rebecca Ann Brown b: May 1999 in Southampton
.....................................7 Sally Elizabeth Brown b: June 2000 in Southampton
.... 6 Sophie Elizabeth Proudler b: November 6, 1983 in Macclesfield
.... 4 Thomas Hall Proudler b: October 10, 1902 in Middlesbrough d: December 1993 in Middlesbrough
...............................+Mabel Bates b: July 25, 1901 in Middlesbrough m: June 1924 in St Michael's, Bakewell, Derbyshire d: April 1999 in
Middlesbrough
.... 5 Audrey Marjorie Proudler b: 1926
.... +Dennis Frisby m: December 1946 in Middlesbrough, Yorkshire
.... 6 Danny Frisby b: Abt. 1950
.....................................5 Dennis H. Proudler b: 1927
..................................+Patricia Plews m: June 1955 in Middlesbrough, Yorkshire
.... 6 Martin JOHN Proudler b: 1958
..................................+Ms Fenimore m: 2000 in Middlesbrough
.... 6 Susan Jane Proudler b: 1958 in 7 august 1958
..................................+Neil Paterson b: 1956 in 14 Dec 1956
.....................................7 Fiona Paterson b: March 1988 in 6 Feb 1988
.... 7 Euan Paterson b: November 1989 in 18 Oct 1989
.... 4 Irene Mary Proudler b: November 22, 1904 in Middlesbrough
.... +William Williamson b: August 31, 1897m: September 1927 in Middlesbrough, Yorkshire
.... 5 David Williamson b: Unknown
.... +Florence ??
.... *2nd Wife of David Williamson:
.... +Linda ??
.... 6 Matthew Williamson b: Unknown
.... 6 Rebecca May Williamson b: Unknown

................................5 Sybil Mary Williamson b: December 24, 1928
.... +Stanley Jackson
.... 6 Beryl Jackson b: June 15, 1951
...................................+Leonard Atess Wilson
.... 7 Neil Wilson b: November 3, 1976
.... 7 Karen Wilson b: March 16, 1982
.... 7 Robert Atess Wilson b: January 8, 1993
.... 6 Susan Jackson b: November 8, 1954
.... 5 Marjorie Williamson b: October 31, 1930
...............................+Jack Claypole
.... 6 Ann Claypole b: April 9, 1958
.... 6 Jill Claypole b: March 23, 1960
...................................+Nigel Dawson
.... 7 Jane Dawson   b: Unknown
.... 7 Nigel Dawson b: Unknown
.... 4 Aubrey William Proudler b: October 13, 1909 d: August 1910 in Middlesbrough
.... 3 Ethel Beatrice Proudler b: 1881 in Sheffield
.... +Jack Price m: June 1906 in Middlesbrough, Yorkshire
.... 4 Stanley Price b: Unknown
.... +Evalin Short
.... 3 Bernard Willie Proudler b: December 22, 1883 in Middlesbrough d: 1978
.... +Margaret Henrietta MacLean b: January 12, 1888 m: January 23, 1909 in Middlesbrough, Yorkshire d: May 22, 1922 in
              Middlesbrough
.... 4 Phillis Emily Proudler   b: February 13, 1909 in Middlesbrough d: March 24, 2001
.... +Albert Palmer b: March 8, 1910 m: December 19, 1931 in Middlesbrough, Yorkshire d: February 20, 1990
.... 5 Denis Palmer b: October 1, 1932
.... +Barbara Bowyer d: Deceased
.... 6 Janet Palmer b: August 1959
.... 6 Carole Palmer b: Abt. 1962
.... 6 Graham Palmer b: Abt. 1966
.... 6 Jonathan Palmer b: Abt. 1968
.............................5 Bernard Palme r b: February 9, 1934
.... +Doris Laing
.... 6 Vicky Palmer b: September 13, 1961
.... 6 Geoffrey Palmer b: Abt. 1965
.............................5 Bryan Palmer b: June 15, 1937
.............................5 Margaret Palmer b: July 12, 1940
.... +Albert Lewis
.... 6 Colin Albert Lewis b: September 29, 1961
.... 6 Steven Andrew Lewis b: October 27, 1962
.... 6 Julie Anne Lewis   b: February 3, 1964
.... +Andrew Pinchbeck m: February 2, 1985
.... 7 Sadie Lee Pinchbeck b: July 19, 1989
....7 Jordan Thomas Pinchbeck b: July 6, 1993
....7 Chloe Louise Pinchbeck b: October 29, 1999
.... 4 Elsie May Proudler b: April 2, 1910 in Middlesbrough d: November 11, 1912 in Middlesbrough
.... 4 Iris May Proudler   b: March 10, 1912 d: May 9, 1915
.... 4 James William Proudler b: February 5, 1915 in Middlesbrough d: March 17, 1948
....   ,,,,,,, +Edna May Rose b: July 26, 1922 m: December 1941 in Middlesbrough, Yorkshire
.... 5 Kenneth William Proudler   b: June 5, 1942
....   ,,,,,,,,,,,,, +Norma Edith Barren b: May 4, 1940 m: June 1963 in Middlesbrough, Yorkshire d: February 12, 1996 in
              Stoke-on Trent
.... 6 Verity Proudler b: June 25, 1966 in Thornaby, Yorks
.... +William A. Venter   m: 1990 in Newcastle under Lyme
.... 7 Jamie Victoria Venter b: June 1993 in Stoke on Trent
.... ,,,, 7 Jared Thomas Venter b: August 1994 in Stoke on Trent
.... 6 Jean Claire Proudler b: March 17, 1968 in Thornaby, Yorks
.... +Anthony D. James   m: November 1988 in Stafford
... ,,,,,,,,,,,,,,,,,   , 7 Benjamin David James b: February 1991
....   , 7 Deborah Bethany G. James b: August 1993
.... 7 Rebekah Anne E. James   b: August 1993
.... 6 Victoria Proudler b: May 3, 1975 in Nuneaton, Warks
...................................+Martin J. Bayley m: 2000 in Stafford
...................................*2nd Wife of Kenneth William Proudler:
...................................+Philippa Ruth Harrison   b: December 28, 1959 in Brigham, Cumbria m: July 1997 in Stafford
...........................5 James Proudler   b: September 9, 1943 in Middlesbrough
...................................+Maureen Temple
.... 6 Karen Ann Lesley Proudler   b: May 2, 1966
...................................+Garry A. Blades m: October 1984 in Cleveland
...................................7 Jonathan Lee Blades b: June 1985

....7 James Kevin Blades b: January 1987
....7 Scott Thomas Blades b: June 1989
....   *2nd Husband of Karen Ann Lesley Proudler:
....+Shaun Martin m: May 1999 in Redcar, Cleveland
....7 Gabriel Cane Martin b: October 1999
....   6 James John Wesley Proudler   b: August 11, 1968 in Middlesbrough
....   +Janice L. Curry m: April 1988 in Doncaster
....   *2nd Wife of James Proudler:
.... +Minnie Anna May O'Hanlon b: September 29, 1952 in Glen Mavis, Scotland m: December 1977 in Cleveland
....   6 Amber Claire Proudler b: March 17, 1985 in Eston, Cleveland
....   4 Doris Jessie Proudler b: March 5, 1917 in Middlesbrough
.... +Raymond William Welburn m: January 1, 1940 in Middlesbrough, Yorkshire d: Bef. 2002
....5 Mavis Sabina Welburn b: January 29, 1941
.... +James Ronald Cooper m: September 3, 1960
....   6 Diane Cooper b: November 10, 1964
....   6 Nigel Cooper b: July 1, 1967
....5 Leonard William Welburn   b: February 24, 1946
.... +Norma Ingrid Ord m: June 7, 1969
....   6Suzanne Ingrid Welburn b: December 12, 1971
....   6 Kristie Louise Welburn b: December 12, 1971
....5 Trevor Welburn   b: February 19, 1948
....+Jean Smith m: August 23, 1969
....   6 Ann Marie Welburn b: July 5, 1971
....   6 Ian Welburn b: March 15, 1973
..................*2nd Wife of Bernard Willie Proudler:
.... +Ethel Parker b: 1895 m: October 1, 1923 in Middlesbrough d: 1971
.... 4 Albert Raymond Proudler b: November 20, 1924 in Middlesbrough   d: September 2004 in Middlesbrough
.... +Edna Grout b: December 7, 1927 in Middlesbrough   m: September 1948 in Middlesbrough, Yorkshire
.... 5 Alan Raymond Proudler b: August 14, 1952 in Middlesbrough
.... +Linda Marie Wilson b: March 3, 1952 in Northallerton m: June 1973 in Teeside
.... 6 Lee Richard Proudler b: September 11, 1974 in Middlesbrough
.... +Michelle Whiley m: August 2001 in Middlesbrough
.... 7 Emily Jane Proudler b: October 2002 in Bristol
.... 7 Katie Louise Proudler b: October 2005 in Bristol
.... 6 Iain James Proudler b: June 1, 1977 in Middlesbrough
.....................5 Barbara Eleanor Proudler   b: August 2, 1958
.... +Derek Lythe m: June 1977 in Cleveland
.... 6 Michelle Louise Lythe b: December 4, 1979 in Middlesbrough
.... 6 Graeme Martyn Lythe b: December 1, 1982 in Middlesbrough
.... 4   Kenneth Proudler b: July 31, 1928 in Middlesbrough d: May 1999 in Middlesbrough
.... +Ivy Parvin m: December 1952 in Middlesbrough, Yorkshire
.....................5 David Proudler   b: November 4, 1952 in Middlesbrough
.... 5 Jean Proudler   b: October 16, 1953
.... +Bernard Meehan b: May 19, 1952   m: June 1978 in Cleveland
.... 6 Michael Meehan b: February 10, 1977
.... 6 Kay Meehan b: October 16, 1978
.....................5 Kathleen Proudler b: January 16, 1955 in Middlesbrough
.... +James Jonesb: January 5, 1954 m: December 1977 in Cleveland
.... 6 Gareth Jones b: May 31, 1978
.... 6 David Jones b: February 8, 1980
.... 6 Emma Jones b: March 24, 1982
.... 5 Colin Proudler b: 1956 in Middlesbrough d: 1976
.... 5 Keith Proudler b: May 16, 1958 in Middlesbrough
.... +Tracy J Canick b: December 20, 1962 m: May 1985 in Cleveland
.... 6 Natalie Jayne Proudler b: December 27, 1987 in Middlesbrough
.... 6 Dale Aaron Proudler b: May 16, 1990 in Middlesbrough
.... 4 Leslie Proudler b: March 11, 1931 in Middlesbrough
.... +Ann Ford
.....................4 Lillian Proudler b: February 13, 1933
.... +Lesley Eliason
.....................*2nd Husband of Lillian Proudler:
.... +Maurice Walmsley   m: December 1952 in Middlesbrough, Yorkshire
.... 4 Cyril Proudler b: December 3, 1936 in Middlesbrough
.... +Lilian Sample m: May 1992 in Cleveland
.................3Florence Emily Proudler b: 1886 in Middlesbrough d: 1939
.................3 Mabel Mary Proudler b: October 4, 1889 in Middlesbrough d: December 24, 1959 in Middlesbrough
.....................+William Dawson b: November 11, 1892 in Middlesbrough m: April 14, 1914 in Middlesbroughd: June 27, 1963 in
                                Middlesbrough
.... 4 Sylvia Dawson b: October 3, 1914 d: December 24, 1989
.... +William Hill m: April 8, 1939

.... 5 Norma Hill b: February 19, 1942
.....................................5 Derek Hill b: August 16, 1946
...........................4 Fred Thomas Dawson b: March 7, 1918 d: November 26, 1985
.... Doris Carter m: November 25, 1939
.... 5 Frederick Thomas Dawson b: August 30, 1940
.... 5 Roy Dawson b: June 11, 1944
.... 6 Paul Dawson b: 1967
....7 a dau Dawson b: Abt. 1995
....7 another dau Dawson b: Abt. 1996
.... 6 Neil Dawson b: 1970
....7 a son Dawson b: Abt. 1995
....7 another son Dawson b: Abt. 1996
.....................................5 Brian Dawson b: April 27, 1957
.... 4 Elsie Dawson b: April 20, 1921 d: March 17, 1999
.... +Bertie Marwood m: July 15, 1946
.................................5 Gillian Marwood b: March 12, 1948
.................................5 Christopher Marwood b: January 19, 1953
.... 4 Margaret Dawson   b: July 27, 1924
.... +Frederick Robinson m: December 14, 1943
.....................................5 Geoffrey Robinson b: November 13, 1945 in Middlesbrough
.....................................5 Jennifer Robinson b: June 24, 1948 in Middlesbrough
.....................................5 Malcolm Robinson b: April 26, 1955 in Middlesbrough
..................3 Fred Cecil Proudler b: 1893 in Middlesbrough d: 1951 in Yorks
................+Lilian Maud Passenger m: September 1920 in Wandsworth
.... 4 Alan F. Proudler-Miller aka John D.A.Miller b: 1928
.... +Carol May Louise Walker m: June 24, 1954 in Wood Green, London
,......................... 5Anthony J.K. Miller b: 1956 in Bournemouth
.... *2nd Wife of Alan F. Proudler-Miller aka John D.A.Miller:
....+Loretta Frances Georgina Belmont m: May 1961 in Middlesex, London
.... 5 Karen Ruth Proudler-Miller b: June 1, 1960
....+Peter Knowles m: 1988
.... 6 Jessica Rose Knowles b: 1989
.... 6 Charlotte Lucy Knowles b: 1991
.... 5 Jonathan Richard Paul Proudler-Miller b: November 11, 1961
.... +Michelle Lester m: 1993
.... 6 Lauren Victoria Proudler-Miller b: 1985
.... 6 Katrina Nicole Proudler-Miller b: 2001
.... 2 Elizabeth Proudler b: March 15, 1863 in Aston Street, Shifnal, Shropshire d: January 17, 1947
.... 2 Sarah Jane Proudler b: July 22, 1866 in High Street, Shifnal d: June 3, 1938 in 18 Whitehill Drive, Brinsworth County, York
..........+Frederick George Wilsonb: June 6, 1870 in Wallington, Wiggenhall, Norfolk m: May 21, 1894 in Parish Church of Wicker,
Sheffield   d: January 7, 1937 in 42 Alma Road Hospital, Rotherham
..................3 John Thomas Wilson b: October 4, 1894 d: July 1895
..................3 Susan Jessie Wilson b: November 19, 1895 d: November 1, 1984
......................+Harry Charlesworth b: February 26, 1896 d: July 7, 1977
..........................4   Lillian M Charlesworth b: 1920
.... +Richard John Shaw b: September 5, 1919 m: January 30, 1943 in Rotherham Parish Church d: October 30, 1990
.... 5 Michael Richard Shaw b: October 10, 1944
.... +Barbara Askey b: March 21, 1950
....   ,,,,,,,,,,   6 Elizabeth Shaw b: February 20, 1977
.... 6 Alison Shaw b. April 30, 1979
..........................4 Winnifred M Charlesworth b: October 22, 1922
.... +Albert Lewis b: September 23, 1922 m: May 18, 1946 in Brinsworth Church, South Yorkshire
.... 5 Margaret Lewis b: June 14, 1951
.... +Philip Varley
.... 6 Stephen Varley b: Unknown
.... ,,,,,,,,,,,,,,,,   6 Darrell Varley b: Unknown
.... ,,,,,,,,,,,,,,,,.....*2nd Husband of Margaret Lewis:
.... ,,,,,,,,,,,,,,.....+Louis Carter
.... ,,,,,,,,,,,,,,,,,,,,,,   6 Simon Carter b: November 25, 1986
.... 4 Kathleen J Charlesworth b: October 27, 1923 d: September 7, 1965
.... +Eric Twigg m: December 25, 1942 d: February 23, 1945 In action.
.... 5 Roy Twigg b: November 3, 1944
...................................+Moira Pearsen b: October 9, 1946
.... 6 Eileen Claire Twigg b: August 24, 1965
.... 6 Bridget Marie Twigg b: September 6, 1967
.... 6 Samantha Rachel Twigg b: October 1, 1970
....   *2nd Husband of Kathleen J Charlesworth:
....   +Wilton Shaw m: 1946
....   5 Valerie Shaw b: July 5, 1950
.... 4 Barbara E Charlesworth b: May 28, 1927

.... +Harold Badger b: October 17, 1920 m: October 30, 1948
.... 5 Susan Elizabeth Badger b: February 17, 1950
.... +John Mowson m: May 22, 1971
.... 6 Karen Elizabeth Mowson b: November 12, 1975
....................................5 Gillian Badger   b: October 1954
.... +David Gibson m: May 13, 1978
.... 6 Stephen David Gibson b: October 11, 1978
.... 6 Vicky Gibson b: August 7, 1981
.... 4 Heather Charlesworth b: September 2, 1929
.... +Jack Shaw
.... *2nd Husband of Heather Charlesworth:
.... +John Seeley Durbin   m: February 22, 1960
.....................................5 Andrew Michael Durbin b: Abt. 1961
....+Jean Stockton
.... 6 Jack Durbin b: May 24, 1997
.... 6 Emma Durbin b: May 24, 1997
..................3 Frederick Tudor Wilson b: November 20, 1902 in Brinsworth, South Yorks d: April 23, 1985 in Good Hope Hospital, Sutton
                    Coldfield, B'ham
........................+Minnie Stanley   b: June 9, 1903 in Rotherham, South Yorks m: May 30, 1925 in Wesleyan Methodist Church, Rotherham,
S.Yorks   d: November 20, 1969 in Good Hope Hospital, Sutton Coldfield, B'ham
...............................4 Gordon Arthur Wilson b: May 13, 1926 d: December 28, 1930 in Whitehill Drive, Brinsworth, Nr Sheffield
...............................4 Barbara Joyce Wilson   b: January 11, 1928
.... +Geoffrey Bryant b: January 29, 1931 m: October 5, 1957
......................................5 Cheryl Patricia Bryant b: May 15, 1959
....+Clint Meehan   b: October 21, 1958   m: in Wylde Green Congregational Church, Sutton Coldfield
.... 6 Robert Patrick Meehan b: June 2, 1986
.... 6 Kirstie Marie Meehan b: December 3, 1987
.... 6 Catherine Alice Meehan b: March 1, 1990
....................................5 Judy Anne Bryant b: February 26, 1961
....................................5 Heather Claire Bryant b: December 7, 1964
.... 6 Willow Anne Bryant b: May 15, 2002
.... 4 Roderick Tudor Wilson b: November 25, 1931
.... +Evelyn Louise Bolan
.... 5 Lynette Wilson b: January 5, 1964
.... +Peter Robert Turner b: July 15, 1965 m: October 24, 1992
.... 6 Jake Turner b: November 1, 1997
.... 6 Lucy Turner b: March 1, 1999
.... 5 Richard Wilson b: January 29, 1966
....................................5 Edmund Wilson b: July 3, 1968
.... 4 Philip Frederick Wilson b: June 3, 1933
.... +Beryl Calvey
.... 5 Karen Elizabeth Wilson b: April 27, 1961
.... +Timothy Heron Walker m: September 14, 1996 in Cogges, Oxfordshire
.... 6 James Heron Walker b: April 22, 1999
.... 6 Edward Walker b: April 16, 2002
....................................5 Gail Yvonne Wilson b: October 10, 1963
....................................5 Ian David Wilson b: November 16, 1966
....................................5 Suzanne Jane Wilson b: November 16, 1966
............................4 Ian Robert Wilson b: May 29, 1939 in Four Oaks, Sutton Coldfield
.... +Cynthia Marylyn Rumball b: November 18, 1939 in Perry Barr m: March 12, 1966 in St Johns, Perry Barr,
                    Birmingham
.... 5 Roger Geoffrey Wilson b: January 9, 1968 in Sutton Coldfield, West Midlands
.... 5 Martin Gregory Wilson b: August 7, 1969 in Sutton Coldfield, West Midlands
....+Louise Marie Sellers b: April 11, 1973m: February 20, 1993 in St Lukes, Scarborough, N. Yorks.
....*2nd Wife of Martin Gregory Wilson:
....+Sheila Morrisey m: May 30, 2003 in Zell-am-Zee, Austria
.... 6 Conor Thomas Wilson b: February 2, 2000
.... 6 Emma Rachel Wilson b: July 18, 2002
.... 6 Daniel Wilson b: December 22, 2003
....................................5 Philip Robert Wilson b: August 7, 1969 in Sutton Coldfield, West Midlands
.... +Debbie Jane Pollard b: December 15, 1970 in Erdington, W.Midlands m: September 19, 1992 in St Michael's
                    Church, Coldmere, Sutton Coldfield
.... 6 Jodie Anne Wilson b: May 16, 1995 in Good Hope Hospital, Sutton Coldfield
.... 6 Kathryn Louise Wilson b: November 4, 1998 in Good Hope Hospital, Sutton Coldfield
.... 2   William Henry Proudler b: 1868 in Shifnal   d: 1934 in Sheffield
....   +Adeline Norton b: 1869 in Yorkshire m: June 1892 in Sheffield   d: 1936 in Sheffield
..................3 John Lawrence Tudor Proudlerb: 1892 in Sheffield   d: 1933 in Sheffield
................+Edith Hodgson   m: September 1911 in Sheffield
......................4   Ronald T. Proudler   b: August 1, 1911 d: November 1992 in Eastbourne
.... +Margaret Knowles b: May 28, 1909 m: September 1933 in Sheffield

```
.....................................5  Jill L.T. Proudler b: 1934 in Eccleshall
.....................................+Alan Cox m: September 1956 in Westminster, London
.............................................  6  Karen Cox b: 1959
.....................................5  Rona M.T. Proudler b: 1937 in Hull
.....................................+Brian Kemp m: September 1961 in Dover, Kent
.............................................  6  Rebecca Kemp b: 1966
.............................................  6  Richard Kemp b: 1968
.....................................5  Zoe M.T. Proudler b: 1943 in Sheffield
.....................................+Anthony Wollaston m: June 1968 in Thanet
.............................................  6  Amy Wollaston b: 1968
.............................................  6  Jay Wollaston b: 1972
.............................................  6  Holly Wollaston b: 1973
..................3  Elsie Sylvia Proudler b: 1894
......................+Mr Barson m: 1941 in Sheffield
..................*2nd Husband of Elsie Sylvia Proudler:
......................+Barson m: March 1941 in Sheffield
..................3  Wilfred Baden Proudler b: 1900 in Sheffield d: 1930
..................3  Mary Proudler        b: 1910
......................+Minnis
```

Children of Thomas Proudler and Mary Tudor

John Proudler 1853-1934

The following article appears in the Northern Daily Mail on Thursday May 17th, 1888:

A PUBLICAN AND HIS WIFE

At Middlesbrough yesterday, John Proudler, landlord of the Ship Launch Inn, Durham Street, was charged with assaulting his wife, Emma Proudler, in Station Street on Friday. Evidence was taken showing that defendant and complainant did not live together, but that the former allowed his wife 15s per week. Last week, however, he did not give her her allowance, but having met her in the street struck her instead. The case was dismissed. John and Emma live separately and a child they had in 1873, not long after they married, seems to die as an infant.

Thomas Proudler 1859-1943

Thomas married Emily Shorthose - see picture right - in December 1879 in Ecclesall. She was born in 1858 and died 1933.
His occupation, according to the various census returns, Varies from being a bricklayer to greengrocer.
They had six children.
(There is a family story that Thomas left the family home in the early 1900s and was not seen again though a "possible" sighting at Emily's funeral — (Source Roy DAWSON) .

Bernard Willie Proudler 1883-1978

Son of the above Thomas and Emily, Bernard Willie marries Ethel PARKER 1895-1971(2nd wife). First wife Margaret McLEAN dies in 1922 from acute rheumatism, and bronchitis, age only 33 yrs. Two children from his first marriage die very young: Elsie May (died aged just 2) – cause shock from burns … She accidentally set herself on fire with matches in her parents' home, accelerated by wearing a flannelette shirt. Also, death of Iris May, aged 3 yrs, died of measles..

Altogether Bernard Willie has ten children; five from his first marriage and five from his second.

Thomas Henry Proudler 1880-1968

Brother of the above, and pictured right, Thomas Henry Proudler was born in 1880 and died 1968. He was Also employed as a bricklayer.

Picture, right, was probably taken about
 1920s-1930s.

Proudlers in Toronto, Canada

The son of Thomas Henry was Maurice Ashmore Proudler 1901-48 who had 8 children; one of whom John Gordon Proudler emigrated to Canada in 1964 and there are descendants there today.

DERBYSHIRE PROUDLERS FROM 1890

As stated at the start of the Yorkshire Proudler section, Thomas Proudler 1797-1832 never leaves Shropshire but current branches of Proudlers (America, Yorkshire and Derbyshire) descend from his children. The Derbyshire branch descend from his daughter Sarah ....

Descendants of Sarah Proudler

1 Sarah Proudler   b: May 23, 1824 in Shifnal, Shropshire
..   +?
........2   Maria Proudler (aka Liza) b: 1843
....   +Thomas Kibble b: 1844 m: June 1866 in Shifnal, Shropshire
..................3 Jane Kibble b: 1867
......................+John Brown b: 1869
.............................4   Mary Elizabeth Brown b: 1897   d: 1967
.................................+David Lindsay Paterson b: 1898 d: 1969
....5 Jean Burns Paterson b: 1927
....+Dennis Simmonds b: 1925
....6 Wendy Simmonds b: 1949 d: 2002 in Leeds
....+Alastair W.M. Hay   b: 1947
....7 Tom Hay b: 1980
.... 6 Malcolm Simmonds b: 1951
....+Mary Skinner b: 1948
....7 Sophie Rose Simmonds   b: 1988
....7 Lydia Ruth Simmonds   b: 1989
.... *2nd Wife of Malcolm Simmonds:
....+Ms Day
....7 Shelley Maria Day b: 1975
.... +David Stillman
....8 Joseph Stillman b: 2001
.... *3rd Wife of Malcolm Simmonds:
....+Ms Lonsdale
....7 Robert James Lonsdale b: 1982
....   5 Robert Paterson b: Unknown
....   5 Ian Fechine Paterson b: Unknown
....   5 Agnes Jane Paterson b: Unknown
....   4 Alfred Brown b: Unknown
....   4 Edith Brown b: Unknown
....   4 Noah Brown b: Unknown
.... 2 Thomas Proudler b: 1846
.... +Mary Sullivan b: 1850 in Ireland   m: 1880 in Kensington, London
.... 3 Cornelius Alfred Proudler b: 1881
.... 3 Jane Ellen Proudler b: 1882
.... 3 Julia Ann Proudler b: 1885
.... 2 Jane Proudler b: 1849
............+?m: 1870 in Shifnal, Salop
..........2 David Proudler b: October 7, 1852 in Shifnal, Shropshire d: June 27, 1927 in Derby (at 58 Great Northern Road, Derby)
.... +Agnes Booth b. 1855 in Wrockwardine Wood m: December 1873 in Shifnal, Shropshire d: 1934 in Derby
.................3 William Proudler   b: June 26, 1874 in Wrockwardine Wood, Shropshire   d: March 4, 1955 in Derby (at 63 Hillcrest Rd, Derby)
.... +Catherine Susan Merrin b: 1875 in Derby m: April 19, 1897 in Registry Office, Derby d: 1957 in Derby (St Thomas Road, Derby)
.... 4 David Frank Proudler (Frank) b: September 16, 1897 in Derby d: February 21, 1966 in Derby (at 2 High Street, Derby)
.... +Dorothy May Mills (Dolly) b: September 10, 1900 in Hackney, London m: September 1923 in Derby d: September 1997 in Derby
................................5 John William Proudler b: December 15, 1923 in Derby d: August 10, 2011 in Derby
.... +Laura Dinsdale b: February 11, 1921 in Darlington m: March 1948 in Derby d: January 1997 in Derby
.... 6 Michael Proudler b: December 23, 1945 in Derby
.... +Diane Hesketh m: March 1974 in Derby
.... 7 Jennifer Proudler b: 1983
.... 6 Graham John Proudler b: July 11, 1949 in Derby
.... +Karen McLean b: July 3, 1958 in Derby m: July 4, 1983 in Derby
.................................5 Ivy Proudler b: 1925 in Derby
..................................+Jeff Rouse
...................................*2nd Husband of Ivy Proudler:

...............................+Ted Sims b: 1923 in Derby m: March 1945 in Derby
.... 6 Anthony D. Sims b: November 1946 in Derby
.... 6 Julie Sims b: November 1951 in Derby
.... +Ken Davison
...................................5 David Frank Proudler b: 1927 in Derby d: November 2004 in Derby
....   +Betty Price m: June 1950 in Derby
....   6 Carole Lesley Proudler b: 1951 in Derby
....+Michael D. Drury m: June 1969 in Derby
....7 Nicholas Paul Drury b: 1972 in Derby
....7 Shelley Drury b: 1974 in Derby
....   +? Finney m: Abt. 1993 in Derby
....8 Hannah Drury (Finney) b: 1994
....   6 Philip D. Proudler   b: 1956
....+Sylvia Fletcher m: June 1979 in Derby
....7 Maxine Elizabeth Proudler b: 1982
...................................*2nd Wife of David Frank Proudler:
.... +Eileen Proudler b: 1939 m: June 1981 in Derby
.... 4 William Proudler b: March 6, 1899 in Derby   d: April 23, 1986 in Derby
.... +Lucy Collopb: February 1901 in Lichfield, Staffs m: September 1925 in Derby d: 1940 in Derby
.... 5 Pamela Proudler b: February 7, 1926 in Derby d: 2004
....   6 David Leslie Proudler b: August 12, 1944 in Derby City Hospital
...................................+Jennifer E. Shirley   m: March 1969 in Basford, Nottingham
....   7 Amanda Elizabeth Proudler b: 1969
....   *2nd Wife of David Leslie Proudler:
.... +Janet I. Sackville m: March 1973 in Derby
....   *3rd Wife of David Leslie Proudler:
.... +Gillian Mottram (Mills) m: February 23, 1980 in Belper, Derbyshire
....7 Penny Proudler b: September 1977
.... 7 Michael David Proudler   b: December 1983 d: December 1983
....   6 Michael Proudler b: 1948
.... *2nd Husband of Pamela Proudler:
.... +Vic ?
....   6 Sharon ? b: Unknown
....   6 Steven ?b: Unknown
.... *3rd Husband of Pamela Proudler:
....   +Jimmy Craw
.... *4th Husband of Pamela Proudler:
.... +Desmond Hills m: September 1947 in Downham, London
.... 5 Sheila Proudler b: February 1, 1927 d: December 2004 in Derby
....   6 Terence Proudler   b: June 1945
....   *2nd Husband of Sheila Proudler:
....   +George William Hargraves b: 1921 m: March 1946 in Derby
....6 Sandra Hargraves   b: Abt. 1947
....7 Katy ? b: 1963
....7 John ? b: 1965
....7   Clare ? b: 1967
....   6 Alan Anthony Hargraves b: Abt. 1949
....   5 Brenda M. Proudler b: 1929 in Derby d: 2005
....   +John A. Dempsey (aka Bill) b: 1921 m: March 1947 in Derby d: 2004 in Derby
....   6 Maureen Dempsey   b: 1948
....+Raymond Thom
....7 Michelle Thom
....7 Patricia Thom
....   6 Patricia Dempsey   b: 1950
....+David Dickson
....7 Melanie Dickson b: Unknown
....7 David Dickson b: Unknown
....7 Samantha Dickson b: Unknown
....   6 Brenda Dempsey b: 1958
....+John Bacon
....7 Michael Bacon
....7 Joanna Bacon
....7 Laura Bacon
....7 Andrew Bacon
....   6 John Dempsey   b: 1953
....+June Pert
....7 Kelly Ann Dempsey
....7 Suzanne Dempsey
....   5 Gordon William Proudler b: 1932
....   +Valerie Ashfield m: December 1961 in Derby

6 Caroline Suzanne Proudler b: 1962 in Derby
6 Richard Gordon Proudler b: 1963 in Derby
+Helen J. Cann m: 1990 in Derby
7 William Joseph Proudler   b: 1995 in Derby
*2nd Wife of Richard Gordon Proudler:
+Justine Barnett m: 1999 in Boston, Lincs
7 Alice Rose Proudler   b: July 2004 in Derby
6 Edward Ian Proudler b: February 28, 1967
+Sarah Binnie m: 1993 in Grantham, Lincs
6 Justine Melonie Proudler b: March 1970 in Derby
+? Cook
7 Chloe Christine V. Cook   b: 1994 in Derby
*2nd Wife of Gordon William Proudler:
+Jean Horvath m: February 1985 in Derby
5 Roy N. Proudler b: 1935
+Dorothy M. Sanders m: March 1959 in Derby
6 Kim E. Proudler b: 1961
+Ian M.Stocker m: September 1981 in Derby
7 Nicole Rose Stocker b: December 1984 in Derby
7 Greg Ian Stocker b: August 1986 in Derby
5 Barry Proudler b: July 1, 1937 d: 2008
+Rose Litchfield b: June 18, 1937 in Derby m: December 1959 in Derby
6 Susan J Proudler b: 1960
6 John B Proudler b: 1961
+Lorraine Doherty m: June 1985 in Derby
7 Mark Antony Proudler b: 1985 in Derby
7 Mark Anthony Proudler b: 1987 in Derby
7 Simon John Proudler b: 1987 in Derby
7 Darrell James Proudler b: 1988 in Derby
*2nd Wife of John B Proudler:
+Helen J. Baggulay m. May 2001 in Erewash
6 Julia A Proudler b: 1963
+Duncan T. Sadler m: May 11, 2002 in Pride Park Stadium, Derby
6 Paul Proudler b: July 8, 1966 in Derby
+Nicola Webster   b: May 14, 1968
7 Luke Paul Proudler b: 2000 in Derby
7 Lucy Rose Proudler b: April 2003
*2nd Wife of Barry Proudler:
+Janet A. Batham m: 2000 in Amber Valley, Derbys
*2nd Wife of William Proudler:
+Lena Shaw b: October 28, 1913 in Lancashire m: September 19, 1942 in Derby Registry Office d: October 8, 2002 in Erewash, Derbyshire
4 Doris Cecillia Proudler b: July 1, 1901 in Derby d: 1982
+William Henry (Harry) Allsopp b: June 28, 1903 in Derby m: December 1921 in Derby d: 1969 in Derby
5 Joyce M. Allsopp b: August 1922 in Derby d: 2008 in Derby
+Ray Woolley m: September 1946 in Derby   d: Abt. 2004 in Derby
6 Jeffrey Woolley b: December 1948 in Derby
+Jennifer m: Abt. 1968 in Stapleford, Derbyshire
7 Adrian Woolley b: Abt. 1970
7 Michael Woolley b: Abt. 1972
5 William T.(Bill) Allsopp b: October 1924 in Derby d: Abt. 2004
+? Lacey
*2nd Wife of William T.(Bill) Allsopp:
+Muriel Lacey   b: Abt. 1925 m. 1952 in Derby   d: Abt. 1960
6 Graham Allsopp b: 1953 in Derby
+?
6 Brian Allsopp b: 1955 in Derby
6 Anthony W. Allsopp b: 1957 in Derby
+Elizabeth M.M. Bennett m: 1980 in Belper, Derbyshire
7 Alistair William Allsopp b: 1985 in Derby
7 Ross Thomas Allsopp b: 1988 in Derby
5 John or Jack H. Allsopp b: June 1927
+Nella M. Humpston m: 1951 in Derby
5 Frederick Allsopp b: August 1931 in Derby d: Bef. 2010
+Hazel Harris m: January 1952 in Derby
6 John F Allsopp b: 1953 in Derby d: Abt. 1958 in Derby
6 Paul F Allsopp b: 1955 in Derby
+Karen J Renshaw m: February 1977 in Derby
6 Ruth E Allsopp b: 1961 in Derby
+Graham T Bruce m: May 1978 in Derby

...........................5 Doris M. Allsopp b: October 1933 in Derby
................................+Brian E Kitching b: 1930 in Derby m: August 1952 in Derby
.... 6 Clinton J. Kitching b: October 1956 in Portsmouth
................................+Kay N. Gilchrist m: December 1979 in Derby
................................7 Nichola Claire Kitching b: May 1981 in Derby
................................7 Rebecca Louise Kitching   b: September 1982 in Derby
.... 6 Hilary Kitching b: February 1958 in Portsmouth
................................+Ashley D. Chilinski m: August 1976 in Derby
................................7 Lucie Anne Chilinski   b: December 1976
.... +Scott Clemens m: March 1999 in Derby
.... 8 Samuel Rhys Clemens b: January 2002 in Derby
................................7 Emma Jane Chilinski b: December 1978 in Derby
................................+Jason M. Simm m: September 1999 in Derby
................................8 Jacob Ashley Simm b: 2000 in Derby
.... 7 Amy Louise Chilinski b: January 1985 in Derby
...........................5 Allan (Jimmy) Allsopp b: November 1935 in Derby
...........................+Vera Hardwidge
...........................5 Sandra Proudler b: December 19, 1943 in Derby City Hospital
...........................+Tom Palmer b: June 9, 1937 in Albert Road, Chaddesden, Derby m: August 28, 1965 in St Mark's, Derby
                           d: February 1990 in Derby
.......................4Florence Beatrice Proudler b: August 6, 1903 in 8 Freehold Street, Derby d: December 21, 1988 in Mackworth, Derby
.......................+Robert Herbert Hartshorn b: January 21, 1903 in Church Street, Ockbrook, Derby. m: September 1926 in Derby
                           d: 1944
.... 5Betty Hartshorn   b: November 4, 1926 in Derby
...........................+John Thomas Ryalls b: 1924 m: September 1948 in Derby d: 2004 in Derby City General Hospital
.... 6 Brenda Ryalls b: May 1952 in Derby
.... +Kevin Potter b: 1952 m: January 1972 in Derby Registry Office
...........................7 Mark Potter b: May 1972 in Derby
.... 7 Amanda Potter b: May 1974 in Derby
.... 6 Steven John Ryalls b: December 1960 in Derby
.... +Lynn Brewin m: September 1986 in Swadlincote, Derbyshire
...........................7 Fiona Ryalls b: December 1990 in Derby
.... 7 Matthew Steven Ryalls b: December 1993 in Derby
.... *2nd Wife of Steven John Ryalls:
...........................+Deborah Anne Cook m: 1999 in South Derbyshire
.... 6 Julie Ryalls b: December 1960 in Derby
...........................*2nd Husband of Florence Beatrice Proudler:
.... +Albert Edward Bradbury b: 1899 m: March 28, 1953 in Derby Registry Office
.......................4 Cecilia Proudler b: September 28, 1906 in Derby d: June 1989 in Derby
.......................+Joseph Hulme b: 1903 m: September 1926 in Derby
...........................5 Vera M Hulme b: 1927 in Derby
...........................+Horace Twell   b: 1922 in Derby m: May 1949 in Derby
.... 6 Edward R. Twell   b: 1954 in Derby
.... +Paula W. Letts m: 1974 in Derby
.... 7 Richard James Twell b: June 1986 in Derby
.... 7 Alastair Geoffrey Twell b: November 1992 in Derby
...........................5 Brian J Hulme b: 1933 in Burton, Staffs
.... +Isobel R. Burton m: 1959 in Derby
.... 6 Kay Hulme b: 1962
.... 6 Sally Hulme b: 1965
...........................7 Ruth Hulme b: 1997
...........................7 Elizabeth Hulme b: 2000
.......................4 Gladys Proudler b: July 9, 1909 in Derby d: April 1986 in Worksop, Notts
.......................+William R. Smith b: December 12, 1905 in Derby m: September 1928 in Derby d: 1989 in Derby
...........................5 Brenda Smith b: November 1933 in Derby
.... +David Holmes m: 1953 in Belper, Derbyshire
.... 6 Paul R Holmes b: 1956 in Derbyshire
...........................+Mary
.... 4 Lucy Muriel Proudler b: February 5, 1912 in Derby d: 1993 in Derby
.... +Henry Greensmith   b: 1912 m: December 1930 in Derby d: 1937 in Derby
...........................5 Jean Greensmith b: 1931
...........................+Thomas E. Johnson m: December 1953 in Derby
.... 6 Stephen Johnson b: December 1957 in Derby
...........................5 Dennis H Greensmith b: 1933 in Derby
...........................+Myrna N. Twigg m: February 1957 in Derby
.... 6 Lesley A Greensmith b: December 1959 in Derby
...........................+Richard O. Goss m: 1991 in St Germans, Cornwall
...........................7 Oliver Percival Goss b: September 1993 in Derby
...........................7 Theodore Benjamin Goss b: May 1996 in Derby
.... 6 Dennis M Greensmith b: May 1963 in Derby

..........................* 2nd Husband of Lucy Muriel Proudler:
.... +Frank W. Hardwidge b: 1910 in Derby m: August 1937 in Derby d: 1987 in Derby
......................5 Vera Hardwidge b: 1938 in Derby
.............................+Allan J. Allsopp b: February 1936 in Derby m: 1957 in Derby
.... 6David A. Allsopp b: 1958 in Derby
.................................+Caron M. Keepin m: 1980 in Derby
....7 Melanie Caron M. Allsopp b: 1981 in Derby
.... 6 Terence Allsopp   b: Unknown
......................5 Tony R Hardwidge b: 1948
............................+Lesley Goodwin m: November 1977 in East Staffordshire
.... 6 Lucy Ann Hardwidge b: 1980
.... 6 Fay Hardwidge b: 1982
.... 6 Lynsey Hardwidge b: 1987 d: October 2005
.... 3 Sarah Jane Proudler b: 1877
.....................+John Richard William Evans m: June 1900 in Derby
..................3 Cecilia Proudler b: 1879
.... +Albert Box b: 1877 in Malmesbury, Wiltshire m: December 1901 in Derby
..................3 Agnes Proudler b: 1885
...................+Thomas John Coxon m: December 1909 in Derby
..................3 Florence Beatrice Proudler b: 1888
.....................+Leonard N. Conway m: June 1916 in Derby
..................3 Lucy Proudler b: 1893 in Derby
...................+William Charles Eyre m: December 1913 in Derby
.... 4 William Charles Eyre b: 1914 d: 1931 in Derby
.... 4 Kenneth T. Eyre b: 1916 in Mar. Q.
.... +Margaret Cahill m: November 1940 in Derby
.... 5 David J. Eyre b: 1941 in Derby
.... 5 James C. Eyre b: 1952 in Derby
.... 4 Lucy Eyre b: 1918 in Sep.Q.
.... +William A. Middleton m: November 1942 in Derby
*2nd Husband of Sarah Proudler:
.+Thomas Lowe b: 1824 in Church Aston, Salop m: June 1855 in Wellington, Shropshire d: 1878 in Shifnal, Salop
.... 2 Ann M. Lowe b: 1847 in Wrockwardine Wood, Salop
.... 2 William George Lowe b: 1848
.... 2 Thomas Lowe b: 1852 in Wrockwardine Wood, Salop
.... 2 Rebecca A. Lowe b: 1856
.... 2 Joseph Lowe b: 1857
.... 2 Henry Lowe   b: 1858 in Nabb, Shropshire
............+Bertha b: 1858 in Oakengates, Shropshire m: 1883 in Wellington, Shropshire
..................3 Nellie Lowe b: in Brightside Bierlow, Sheffield
..................3 Frances Lowe b: in Brightside Bierlow, Sheffield
..................3 Jessie Lowe b: in Brightside Bierlow, Sheffield
.... 2 John Lowe b: 1860
............+Elizabeth b: 1862 in Newport, Salop m: 1886
..................3 Elizabeth M. J. Lowe b: 1886 in Wellington
..................3 Horace J. Lowe b: 1888 in Wellington
..................3 Mary A. Lowe b: 1891 in Wakefield
..................3 Eveline Lowe b: 1894 in W. Derby
..................3 Harry Lowe b: 1898 in W. Derby
.... 2   Sarah J. Lowe b: 1862
.... 2   George H. Lowe b: 1864 in Nabb, Staffs
....   +Beatrice Wardell m: 1894 in Derby
.... 2   Alfred Lowe b: 1866 d: 1875 in Shifnal, Salop
.... 2   William Lowe b: 1868

PROUDLERs arrive in Derby 1890

David PROUDLER 1852-1927

Sarah's son David is born in Shropshire and
marries Agnes Booth there. Five of their six
children they have are born there before, in 1890,
they move to Derby and are to be found on the
1891census living at <u>58 Great Northern Road</u>

(pictured right). David is still there at his death in 1927. In this small terraced house, David lived with wife Agnes and six children. They also had a long-term lodger (Edwin Nuckle) who is living with the family on both the 1901 and 1911 census. They also had a lodger in 1891 (Harry Watson).

It is not known whether Sarah came with her son to Derby as her death record has not been found, though it is thought she may have remained in Shropshire. The reason for the family moving to Derby is not clear - though employment opportunities might be one reason. However, it is thought that David's son William (who would only have been 16 years old in 1890 when they moved, had probably already met his future wife (Kate) in Shropshire and Kate's family were from Spondon, Derby. Kate had apparently been working in domestic service in Shropshire. So, maybe Kate's family connection with

Derby was somehow behind the Proudler family moving there. Census returns show that David worked as a bricklayer and died of bronchitis. He is buried at Nottingham Road Cemetery. He is buried with wife Agnes in plot number 3860 which is a family burial plot purchased for 100 years; David being buried there in 1927 the burial rights expire 2027. The location is termed a "First Class" plot located near the main entrance. Also buried in the same plot is grand-child William Charles Eyre. William had worked for the Trent Motor Traction Company as a Motor Engineer and died very young. Work colleagues put a vase on the grave dedicated to his memory.

So David married Agnes Booth and they had six children. It is from their eldest child, William - the only male - that all the Derby Proudlers descend:-

David & Agnes

William	Sarah Jane	Cecilia	Agnes	Florence Beatrice	Lucy
1874-1955	b.1877	1879-1972	1885-1964	1888-1957	1893-1951
Wrockwardine	Wrockwardine	Wrockwardine	Wrockwardine	Wrockwardine	Derby
Shropshire	Shropshire	Shropshire	Shropshire	Shropshire	

William 1874-1955 There is a whole section (below) dedicated to William.
Sarah Jane b. 1877 - it is not known what becomes of Sarah Jane, other than the fact that she marries John Richard William Evans in 1900 Derby.
Cecilia 1879-1972 marries Albert Box - a Police Constable - and they leave Derby between 1903-1909. They have three sons and lived in Wiltshire. Their address on the 1911 census was The Common, Holt, Nr Trowbridge, Wiltshire. Cecilia dies in 1972 in Bath.

Agnes b. 1885 married Thomas John Coxon and, on the 1911 census, she and her husband are living with her family at 58 Great Northern Road. (Proadley - is the incorrect name that the Proudlers are listed under on that census). Agnes is working as a hosiery forewoman. Agnes dies in 1964 and the couple do not appear to have had any children.

Florence Beatrice 1888-1957 marries Leonard Conway in 1916 and it is not thought they had any children. Leonard served in the Royal Army Service Corps and was awarded the Victory Medal.

Lucy 1893-1951 marries William C Eyre 1889-1971. They have three children. The eldest child William Charles P Eyre 1914-31 died young and is buried with his grandparents at the Nottingham Road Cemetery in Derby in a family grave.

David's son William then is responsible for the Proudler name in Derby. William will have seven children, five girls and two boys. The two boys, David Frank and William will form two separate lines of Proudler descent in Derby. But first, some information about William Proudler (senior) .....

William Proudler 1874-1955

William (1874-1955) 'Bill' , took some time to settle in Derby as the census returns and family birth/marriage certificates and electoral rolls show various addresses through the years:

1874	**SHROPSHIRE** – born Wrockwardine, Shropshire.
1890	**DERBY** – Family leave Shropshire and arrive in Derby
1891	58 Great Northern Road – family home
1897	64 Great Northern Road – wife's address at marriage
1898	Chapel Lane, Spondon (wife's parent's home) address 1st child born
1899	63 Great Northern Road – address when 2nd child born
1901-2	86 Moss Street – address when daughter Doris Cecilia is born (from census)
1903-10	8 Freehold Street – address at daughter Florence Beatrice's birth (from census)
1911	260 Stockbrook Street – address from 1911 census
1916	Feb 15th 6 Court 4 House, Abbey Street – address at army enlistment 15 Feb 1916
1916	Aug - 20 Becket Well Lane (one daughter lived at number 12)
1916–19	WWII War Service (UK based: Yorks/Durham/Ripon/Northumberland)
1933-53	3 Becket Well Lane (address on the 1933 electoral roll & wedding 1953)
1953-55	63 Hillcrest Road – address on death certificate

1955-1957   After Bills death, wife Kate leaves Hillcrest and goes to live with daughter Cissy at St Thomas Road Derby. Kate, within two years, dies at this location.

Pictured right: William Proudler (1874-1955)

Taken at Becket Well Lane, Derby, early 1950s
Picture supplied by Jeffrey Woolley
(Bill's great-grandson).

Proudler Household

BECKET WELL LANE, DERBY

The above picture was sent to us by Jeffrey WOOLLEY (grandson of Doris Cecilia PROUDLER 1901-1982) and appeared in the Derby Evening Telegraph about 1969-1970. The caption under the picture reads ...... "These congested dwellings in Becket Well Lane, Derby, were demolished in 1960". In his capacity as a bricklayer/builder, Bill was occasionally called upon to repair some of the above properties.

The PROUDLERs had vacated the area early in the 1950s in a forced clearance and it is perhaps likely that the houses were empty for some years before demolition. On the left of the above picture, can be seen house with no window frames and, on the right, the sign of the Ford Company.

Grand-daughter Lucy PROUDLER lived on the houses to the left of this picture. There was a shop on the left nearside of picture, as indeed was Fords right nearside.

Bill's longest lived at address was at Becket Well Lane and, over the years, his children also occupy houses in this area – daughter Lucy and her family living at no. 12 and William himself initially at number 20, then later at number 3. Daughter Florence Beatrice PROUDLER's second husband Albert Bradbury also records his address at marriage as being 22 Becket Well Lane (they marry in 1953). This area is now in Derby City Centre and has been developed.

The Becket Well Lane area was so-called because of claims that Thomas-a-Becket visited or stayed in the area and the housing was built around the Well. These houses were just one room down-stairs, one room upstairs and an attic. No indoor plumbing; instead communal wash house blocks a short distance away.

PROUDLERs were rehoused from here about 1950, as the area was cleared (slum clearance) to make way for a new shopping precinct – Duckworth Square – itself now demolished.

Bill's fiddles ...

Bill had a passion for music - a piano was squeezed into their tiny overcrowded house and, in prominent place over the mantle place there were his fiddles. He had three; two of which have been passed down through different branches of the family. Grandson, John William PROUDLER– Jack (1923-2011), recalled his grandfather, playing the fiddle in the street in the Becket Well Lane area, putting his cap on the ground and, when the pennies started to mount up – as soon as there was enough, he would be off to the local pub. Grandson Brian HULME also recalls this, saying that he (as a child) would sit outside drinking lemonade and eating crisps at The Scarsdale Arms (on Colyear Street) whilst Bill was inside playing his fiddle.

An article appeared in the Derby Daily Telegraph on Monday 29th August 1921 as follows:

> *BRITISH LEGION, SADLER-GATE BRANCH*
> *Another fine concert was given on Sunday night and was a huge success. The*
> *artists responsible for the pleasant evening were Mr T Chapman's string band,*
> *assisted by Mr S Walker Jnr piano selections and Mr S Perry, songs by Mr Walding*
> *(comedian), Mrs Milner, Guardsman Clarke, Mr T Chapman (cornet solo) and*
> ***Mr Proudler (one string violin)**. The chair was taken by Mr W Paulson who, at the*
> *close of the concert moved a hearty vote of thanks to the artists. This was seconded*
> *by Mr A S Dean.*

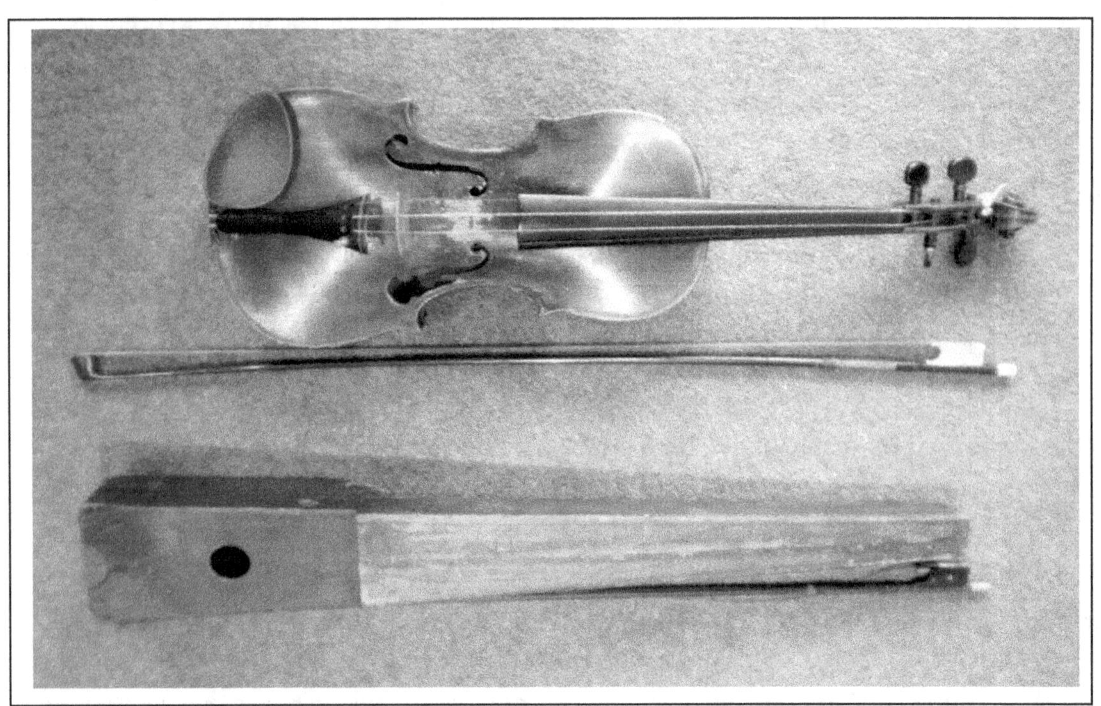

**Top (violin) belongs to grand-daughter Doris KITCHING;
underneath (fiddle) belongs to grand-daughter Sandra PALMER
Violin and fiddle reunited (after some 55 years) for this photograph**

Bill's violin, in the possession of grand-daughter Doris KITCHING for the last 40 years, was passed along the ALLSOPP line of the family. From Doris Cecilia ALLSOPP (nee PROUDLER) to her daughter Joyce. Then from Joyce to the present "Keeper" Doris.

Grand-daughter Sandra (PALMER) – "Keeper" of Bill's Fiddle describes how they were displayed above the family fireplace in Becket Well Lane for many years. Grand-daughter Betty RYALLS (nee HARTSHORN) recalled Bill having three string instruments: a base, a standard violin and a one-string fiddle made from cigar boxes – she identified the above one-string fiddle as the last of these. She remembers having to find "A" on the piano for Bill to tune it. Another grand-daughter Brenda HOLMES remembers the piano as being perhaps walnut with two candlesticks – one either end. Betty also says Bill did play the theatre (Hippodrome or the Grand on Babbington Lane) for quite some time as an entertainer and was often to be found rehearsing etc. She believes that the base instrument was sold to The Grand.

Military Service - WWI Army Service Numbers: 187759 (59670)

William enlists (or was drafted) on 15 February 1916 at the Normanton Barracks in Derby - Army Form B. 2512. From records at the National Archives can be seen the paperwork he was issued on the day ....
"Received from the Recruiting Officer, Normanton Barracks, Armlet No. 690/45, also one leaflet." His age at enlistment was 39 yrs and 8 months; the age range for conscripts in World War I was 18-41 years, so he was at the top end of the range.   Address at enlistment was 6 Court 4 House, Abbey Street,

Derby. Place of birth Wrockwardine Wood, Shropshire (wrongly recorded as Rockwood Iron Wood, Salop) by someone who obviously was not familiar with the place name. Occupation: bricklayer.

Medically examined on 25 August 1916
Height 5' 8¼"; chest 36.5 inches with 2 inch expansion.   Weight 145 lbs (10.4 stones).
Vision: slight defect, but not sufficient to cause rejection.
Next of kin: Catherine Susan, 6 Court 4 House Abbey Street, Derby. Married: Registry Office Derby, 1898.
Children: Doris, Florence, Cecilia, Gladys and Lucy (girls only listed, not the two boys – who were maybe considered adults, i.e. not dependents). It appears, from his Statement of Service, that all of William's Army Service was in the UK, probably he was labouring on military sites:
Regiment: 345 Newcastle; Regiment: 357 Ripon Camp; Regiment: 355 Grantham

Statement of Service

15 Feb 1916	1 day	Enlisted at Derby	Army rank Private General Service
16 Feb 1916	190 days	To Army Reserve	
24 Aug 1916		Mobilized to depot Infantry Works Company West Yorks Regiment	
28 Aug 1916		Service reckoned from D of W. £2-25sh	Mobilised, terms of service Posted Durham Light Infantry
1 Sep 1916		Transferred Labour Corps	Transferred from Depot, Yorks Private
1 Sep 1916			Posted Durham Light Infantry
15 Dec 1916		Attested	Private
16 Dec 1916		To Army Reserve Labour Corps – 3rd Battn.	Private 1917 R.C.D.
13 Jan 1917		Absent without permission from 13 Jan 1917 4am till 15 Jan 1917 at 3pm	Forfeited pay
Feb 1917		Absent without permission From 23 Feb to 27 Feb	Forfeited 5 days pay
28 Apr 1917		A.C.I.? C.R.& C.	
1 June 1917		Posted Labour Battn.	7th Battn/Depot.
24 June 1917		Posted Home Service Company	
30 July 1918 to		Absent without permission (confined to barracks)	Punishment: 14 days C.B.
10 Aug 1918		Place: Cambois, Private Northumberland	Punishment: 14 days C.B. – confined to barracks; docked 14 days pay
10 Aug 1918		Rejoined 2pm	
12 Nov 1918		Posted 355 Battn.	Home Service Works Corps 357 & 345
30 Jan 1919		W. Labour Centre, N.C.	Grantham, Lincs
30 Jan 1919		Proceed to Labour Centre, Ripon for dispersal under demobilisation service reckoned from ...28.8.1916 355 Home Service Works Co.	

1 Feb 1919	Declaration that he is not suffering disability due to war service.
5 Feb 1919	Protection Certificate issued &
	Certificate of Identity
	Granted 28 days furlough
5 Mar 1919	Army reserve on demobilisation,
	Character: good

Did not claim to be disabled as a result of service in war at 1919, medically examined at Belton Park, Grantham 1 Feb 1919. Unit attached to: 355 (Home Service) Works Company.
Home address: 20 Becket Well Lane, Derby

Place of joining: Ripon; theatre of war or command Northern, medical category B2.
Address in 5 March 1919: 20 Becket Well Lane, Derby

The Ripon Camp that Bill was sent to was a large military encampment constructed during 1915 on the outskirts of Ripon in Yorkshire which acted as a logistical centre for assembling troops to be despatched to, or returning from, the front lines. The camp also contained a Prisoner of War camp.

The Labour Corps (otherwise known as the H.S. Corp – Home Service Corp) was sometimes regarded as being for those who were not fit enough or young enough for front line fighting. Bill, at the top end of the age range, was assigned as being fit for Labour Corps. The regiment he was assigned to – the Durham Light Infantry - did send half its regiments to fight in France in 1916 at the Somme, but Bill's particular regiments were UK based only.

In 1917 Bill goes AWOL absent without official leave on two occasions, and then in 1918 for the third time he is AWOL, this time for 10 days – for which he is punished (C.B. – confined to barracks/pay docked).

Pictured right is 63 Hillcrest Road, Derby – address at William (Bill's) death.

This is where the family would have been moved to after they were rehoused when the Becket Well Lane area was cleared and developed, but not for long. Kate, in particular, was never happy living here as she missed her previous town-centre home at Becket Well Lane. William (Bill) PROUDLER dies here and immediately afterwards, the family decide that Kate (Catherine Susan Merrin) should live with one of them and, as Cissy had a spare room at the time, Cissy took her in. Cissy and husband Jo HULME lived at the top of

St Thomas Road, Derby (near to the Normanton Barracks) and they had a flat over a shop.

Jo HULME ran a pawnbrokers business and this is where Kate spent her final days, she died within two years of her husband and whilst living at St Thomas Road, Derby.

The following reminiscences are from Brenda HOLMES (b. 1933) - Catherine's grand-daughter, daughter of Gladys PROUDLER 1909-1986. Brenda used to visit her PROUDLER grandparents at Becket Well Lane when she was young (usually on a Saturday when shopping with her mother so this would perhaps be the 1940s and early 1950s) and would often ask Kate about her early times and Shropshire .....

Kate told Brenda about how she met Bill PROUDLER (1874-1955) in Shropshire. Kate was from a Derby family (the MERRINS in Spondon) and, after her mother Ann's early death (1842-1883) during child-birth, Kate and some siblings were placed in domestic service and, in Kate's case, she was sent to work at a vicarage in Shropshire. It is possible that it was the vicarage at St Peter's Priorslee as that would have been close to where the PROUDLERs were living at the time (late 1880s). Kate described living in-service at the vicarage where there were seven sons in the household – she would, at night, wedge a chair under her bedroom door handle, so no one could enter the room after dark – although it seems to have been the parson that pestered her rather than the sons. She was initially employed to clean the house which sometimes included the kitchens and, as she got to know the cook she would ask to do some cooking and learned cooking skills. When the elderly cook decided to retire she recommended Kate to take over, which she did.

One day a local bricklayer was called to do some work at the vicarage, that bricklayer was William (Bill) PROUDLER and that is how they met. Kate initially rebuffed him, saying he had dirty fingernails.   It is not known exactly what happens next, whether it was Kate that was instrumental in Bill PROUDLER's family leaving Shropshire and moving to Derby, but her arrival in Shropshire in the late 1880s, does coincide some short time later with the PROUDLER's decision to move to Derby in 1890. It is known that the first PROUDLERs, Bill's father David and family, lived at 58 Great Northern Road and, interestingly, Kate puts her address at marriage in 1897 as being 64 Great Northern Road. So perhaps the families' relationship between Kate and Bill led to the MERRIN and PROUDLER families becoming acquainted and this precipitated PROUDLERs moving to Derby at this time.

The couple are at various addresses during their early marriage and, it isn't until after Bill's service in WWI, that they settle at Becket Well Lane where they remain for the following 30+ years.

Bill's work as a bricklayer could potentially leave him huge periods of unemployment in the winter months.   If it was too cold for the mortar to set, then he couldn't work for weeks or months on end. And, in those circumstances, he would have been entitled to only 10 shillings per week for the entire family to live on. Kate took in laundry for a local woman to help out.

Bill was a master bricklayer, often being called in to do jobs that others were not able to. It is known that he worked on many of the houses in the Broadway district north of Derby – which is still today a very affluent area with many large houses.

Daughter Lucy and her family lived at the top end of Becket Well Lane and Kate would also help in bringing up these grandchildren too. Kate would cook kippers and pieclets every Saturday evening and always invited family to their house – even though there was not much space.

Kate used to tell Bill off as he frequently, clumsily, damaged the gas mantles (by putting his thumb through them) – mantles used for the gas lighting. He also used to annoy Kate by performing tricks – balancing her freshly baked small cakes on the back of his wrist and flick them over to (hopefully) catch them in his hands. Bill affectionately referred to Kate as "woman". Kate seemed to be always working, always wearing an apron, never seeming to take holidays or go out – always on the go working in the home. She always wore a long black dress and hair in a bob with a bone fitting through it and flat shoes. Gardens at the houses in Becket Well Lane were communal yards and the women would take it in turns each day to hang out washing – Kate's day was Wednesday.

Brenda describes the local shops; a Miss PORTER's sweet shop nearby, also in Macklin Street a shop run by a Mrs SHARROTTS (who had married an American soldier) who sold home-made ice-cream. Kate would send Brenda to the shop with a bowl (before cornets were invented) and get the bowl filled up with ice-cream. Similarly, at another shop – GREENS – Brenda was sent to get steak and kidney pies, again the bowl was taken and she would ask for gravy in it.

Sometimes Brenda would brush Kate's hair for her – it was long, grey, waist-length hair which she never wore down, it was always worn up in a bun. Kate did not smoke or drink and Brenda said she was perhaps rotund, but not fat. Both Kate and Bill die of old age and Brenda recalls Kate crying a great deal and being beside herself for many weeks after Bill's demise. Kate leaves Hillcrest after her husband's death and moves in with daughter Cissy (who had a spare room) at St Thomas's Road, Derby. Sadly within two years Kate dies here. Grandson Brian HULME recalls hearing how Kate, during thunderstorms at Becket Well Lane would sit at the top of the stairs, open doors to allow thunderbolts to pass through, after wrapping the cutlery in an oil cloth and put a damp cloth on her head! Brian had the room next to Kate's at St Thomas's Road but was away serving in the RAF when Kate died.

* * * * * * * * * * *

The Merrin Ladies .....

Ann MERRIN (nee SIMS) 1842-1883
Picture right: taken 1861
Occupation: Lace worker, Spondon, Derby
Bill's mother-in-law

Special thanks to Brenda HOLMES
(great-grand-daughter) for supplying this photo.
The picture was for some years kept by
Cissy PROUDLER, then passed to Gladys,
then finally to daughter Brenda.

These two pictures are mother and daughter.
Ann (right) was the mother of Catherine Susan
Merrin (right)

William/<u>Bill</u> Proudler married CATHERINE /<u>Kate</u>
SUSAN MERRIN on April 19, 1897 in
Registry Office, Derby, daughter of
CHARLES MERRIN and ANN SIMS.
Catherine was born 1875 in Derby and died
1957 in Derby (St Thomas Road)·

William and Catherine (Kate) are both
buried at Nottingham Road Cemetery
in Derby in unmarked graves.
William's occupation: Bricklayer
Died of heart failure/arteriosclerosis &
senility.

Catherine's picture was taken on 21 February
1939 at JEROME's Photographic Studio,
26 Victoria Street, Derby

Ann Merrin 1842-1883

Catherine Susan Merrin 1875-1957

Photograph is on a postcard, date stamped. Would have cost 10d (4p) – there was a 30 minute wait
after picture taken to it being ready.

Special thanks to Vera and Brian Hulme (Kate's grandchildren) for supplying this photo).

Children of Bill and Kate Proudler

Starting with the eldest, David <u>Frank</u>, we will now look at each line of descent from Bill and Kate. Frank and William, the two boys and the eldest, form two separate lines to continue the Proudler name in Derby.

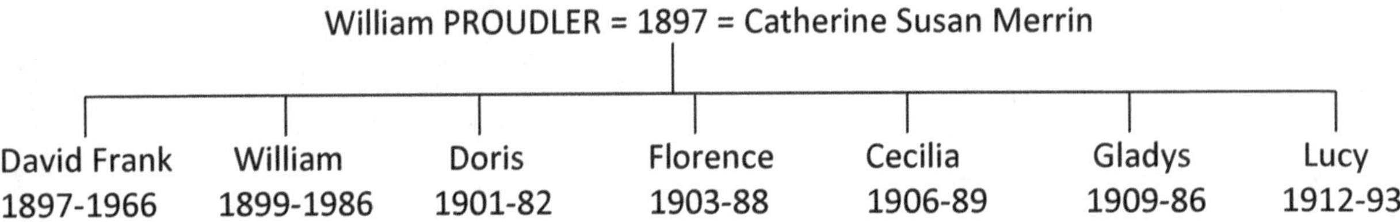

William PROUDLER = 1897 = Catherine Susan Merrin

David Frank	William	Doris	Florence	Cecilia	Gladys	Lucy
1897-1966	1899-1986	1901-82	1903-88	1906-89	1909-86	1912-93

David <u>Frank</u> Proudler 1897-1966

Frank was the second Proudler to be born in Derby and, according to the 1911 census, he was born at Chapel Lane, Spondon (his mother's Merrin family home) whereas younger brother William was born at Great Northern Road (father's family home).

Frank was awarded two medals for his service in World War I: The Victory Medal, and The British Medal and he served with the following regiments as a Private:

    West Yorkshire – regiment number 58034,
    South Yorkshire – regiment number 51250, and
    Notts & Derby – regiment number 125385.

He worked for British Rail in Derby (outside and no. 1 shop) as an electrician's mate. Both of his sons would follow him into the employ of British Rail where they would spend the whole of their working lives. Frank lived at 2 High Street in Derby; High Street itself has disappeared now as the area has been redeveloped - though an archive picture has been found ....

High Street pictured right. Looking from London Road end up towards Royal Crown Derby (chimney) in distance. Bob Minnion Motor Bike Shop is left corner. High Street was located near to St Andrew's Church on London Road (which has also been demolished) and close to Derby railway station. Part of High Street was bombed in the Second World War on 19th August 1940 when the Proudlers were living there.

Frank married Dolly in September 1923, but by December 1923 she had given birth to their eldest John William (Jack) Proudler. Pictured below, wife Dorothy MILLS (1900-1997) with two children: Jack (1923-2011) and Ivy (1925-2009). Picture dated 1932. *(Big thank you to Julie DAVISON -nee SIMS for providing photos – Julie is Ivy PROUDLER's daughter).* Youngest son Frank ran off (camera shy) when this picture was taken.

Grand-daughter Julie (SIMS) believes that David <u>Frank's</u> cause of death was related to his being "gassed" in the First World War.

Children of Frank and Dolly

John William (Jack PROUDLER 1923-2011)

An article appeared in the Derby Evening Telegraph on Monday February 22nd, 1937. "DERBY BOY FOOTBALLER HURT - While playing football for St James's Church Boys on Saturday, Jack Proudler (13) of 2 High Street, Derby, was struck on the right eye with the ball. He was taken to the Derbyshire Royal Infirmary and detained."
Picture right of Jack... inscription
"To My Dearest Laura". [Laura PROUDLER, nee DINSDALE]

Son of David Frank PROUDLER (1897-1966) Jack was a life-long worker at Derby Railway Works. The picture below was taken circa 1970 at his retirement; some 40 years later his employment at British Rail was to ultimately shorten his life. Number 8 shop, where Jack worked, was continuously exposed to asbestos dust causing his premature death from asbestosis.

Jack is on the middle row second from the right ....
Jack married Laura Dinsdale in 1948 after the birth of their son Michael in 1945. (Laura had been previously married to Stanley Quintin in 1942).

LAURA DINSDALE (1921-1997)

Laura used to tell a story about being chased down Vale Street in Derby[6], during the Second World War, by a Nazi plane which was shooting at her. She hid in what she called Scattergood's entry *(a house across the road from her home at the time),* and son Graham recalls being shown the bullet holes in the building many years later.

Picture left: 32 Crewe Street Derby (Jack/Laura's home) They had previously lived at Vale Street (rented from "Auntie" Fannie[7] (Laura had lived there when posted to the area in WWII.
Picture right: Laura (left) with mother-in-law Dolly.

---

[6] Derby, with its Rolls Royce engine aircraft industry was a prime target and so the town was ringed with aircraft guns, search lights and barrage balloons in World War II.

[7] Son Graham remembers a Mrs Bull, two doors away at an off-licence. You took your own bottle and they filled it with Charringtons Beer (a local beer maker on Peartree Road, Derby)

As part of the Derby Museum's Millennium Celebrations, the following news article was printed which confirms Laura's story ....

"NEWS IN BRIEF: CIVILIANS SHOT BY ENEMY AIRCRAFT

Monday 27th July 1942

Twenty-two civilians were killed and many more injured in a terrifying attack by a lone enemy aircraft today. At 7.50 am the Dornier 217 skimmed the roof tops of Rolls-Royce with bomb doors open and machine guns blazing. Two bombs caused considerable damage to stores, workshops and houses opposite the works. The aircraft then turned its attention to Osmaston Road and surrounding streets where it gunned down workers. It then flew towards Friar Gate area where the Babbington Lane barrage balloon was shot down and a bus in Slack Lane machine-gunned".

Laura Proudler, dressed in her army uniform, was spotted by the plane and shot at. Her location would have been right on the plane's path, after leaving Rolls Royce, it would have flown over Vale Street on its way to Friar Gate.

Betty HARTSHORN also recalls this incident as she walked to Rowleys Hosiery Works on Uttoxeter Road, she was also shot at and recalls someone pushing her into Monk Street air-raid shelter for safety. Betty also recalls, some years earlier, as a 13 year old at Gerrard Street School, seeing the skies above her filled with aircraft (this would have been 1940 Battle of Britain year).

Children of Jack and Laura Proudler

Graham Proudler (b. 1949)
Picture right: Son of John William Proudler (1923-2011) and wife Karen.
Graham worked for 25 years for Derby County Football Club as Training Ground Manager initially at The Ramarena on Raynesway (now demolished) and then oversaw the construction of the new multi-million pound facilities at Oakwood where he was the first Manager.
He married Karen (nee McLEAN) in 1983.
When Graham first arrived at Derby County Football Club, Peter TAYLOR was Manager.
Then, others followed ... Roy MacFARLAND, Arthur COX, Billy McEWAN, Jim SMITH, Colin TODD, John GREGORY and George BURLEY.

Right: Graham holding the F.A. Cup.

Jack and Laura had an older son Michael, b. 1945 who is married with a daughter.

Ivy Proudler 1925-2009

Daughter of Frank and Dolly Proudler, Ivy married Ted Sims in 1945 and had two children: Anthony and Julie. Later in life, after Ted's demise, she married Godfrey Rouse.

Frank Proudler 1927-2004

DERBY EVENING TELEGRAPH, MONDAY, JANUARY 29, 1945

Signalman E. J. Sims and his bride, Miss Ivy Proudler

MARRIED WHILE ON LEAVE

Signalman E. J. Sims, home on leave from B.L.A., son of Mr. and Mrs. H. Sims, of 32, Yates-street, Derby, was married to Miss Ivy Proudler, daughter of Mr. and Mrs D. F. Proudler, of 2, High-street, Derby, at St. Andrew's Church, Derby, on Saturday.

The best man was Mr. H. Sims, and Miss M. Stevens and Miss J. Harwood were the

No Electricity Cut, But—

DERBY Power Station manged to "struggle through" this morning without shutting down on any district, Mr. F. H. Pooles, the Borough Electrical Engineer, told a "Telegraph" re-

WEDDING OF DAVID <u>FRANK</u> PROUDLER (1927-2004)TO BETTY ON 10th JUNE 1950

**Thanks to Lesley (Frank and Betty PROUDLER's daughter) for the above picture.*
Left to right: John William PROUDLER (b. 1923-2011) holding baby Graham John PROUDLER (b. 11.7.49-); Ivy PROUDLER (1925-2009); Laura PROUDLER (nee DINSDALE) (wife of John William) (1921-1997); David Frank PROUDLER (1927-2004)groom; Betty PRICE (bride); Bessy WALLBANK (bride's cousin), groom's friend "flap", then William PRICE (bride's father), Dorothy PROUDLER (1900-1998), David Frank PROUDLER (1897-1966); boy at front Michael PROUDLER (b. 1945).

Children of Frank and Dolly

Next, we return to the second branch of Proudlers in Derby who descend from David <u>Frank</u> Proudler, that is the second son William.

William PROUDLER (1899-1986)

William PROUDLER is pictured in 1941 at East Street, Derby selling flowers – outside Williamsons Cafe. Niece Betty RYALLS (HARTSHORN) recalls "Uncle Bill" carrying flower baskets on his head; she would go to Woolworths to buy little jars of Palm of Violets which Bill would sprinkle over the flowers to make them smell nicer/fresher *Thank you to youngest daughter Sandra for supplying this picture.*

1899-1900	63 Great Northern Road, Derby (across the road from grandparents)
1901	86 Moss Street, Derby (1901 census)
1916	4th August – Enlisted WWI - gave his family's address as 20 Becket Well Lane
1916-1924	Marine – WWI (initially based at Deal in Kent) and on board at least 3 ships
1924	August – invalided out of the Royal Marines
1925	First marriage - to Lucy COLLOP in September 1925
1926	12 Becket Well Lane, Derby (at daughter Pamela's birth).
1933	Parents' address on 1933 electoral roll is 3 Becket Well Lane
1940	35 Carter Street, Derby (at wife Lucy's death).
1942	Marriage to 2nd wife Lena SHAW, same address.
1943	Birth of last child, daughter Sandra, still at 35 Carter Street.
1944-50	1 William Street (former Old Dove Inn)
1950-51	Wisbech, Cambs
1951-52	3 Becket Well Lane (lived with parents for a few months)
1954-65	129 Green Lane, Derby
1965-1986	Green Lane/Crompton Street, then lastly Borrowash.

William's birth certificate states that he was born at 63 Great Northern Road. His grandparents (David & Agnes) were living at no. 58 (where they continued to live until their deaths many years later). So either the birth certificate is wrong (which seems unlikely), or Williams father (William 1874-1955) must have briefly resided at no. 63. The 1901 census shows the family living in Moss Street and another family (The PEATS) living at no. 63 Great Northern Road, so their tenure must have been short – a year or two maximum.

On his enlistment papers, in 1916, curiously he refers to his mother as Kathleen (Catherine Susan MERRIN).

William served in the First World War as a Marine and his military service record has recently been released by the National Archives. He enlisted in August 1916 when he was under-age and spent the first year (Aug 1916 to Jul 1917) at the naval training depot in Deal, Kent. He was later to serve on at least three ships which were stationed in the main in the Mediterranean and Black Sea areas – see military record which follows. His first enlistment ends early/mid 1922. It is suspected that he spent one year 1922/23 working as a bricklayer's labourer as he states that to be his occupation when enlisting for a second time on 18 September 1924. However, within months of this second period of service, he appears to sustain an injury; his record shows him being in receipt of a payment for "wounds and hurts" on 11 Jan 1924 before his final "invalid discharge" in April 1924.
He marries within one year of leaving his military service in 1925.

William PROUDLER 1899-1986

Above right: here he is pictured at the Festival of Britain in 1951. It is believed he was there for several months, possibly for the duration of the Festival – which ran from 3 May to 30 September 1951.

The Festival was designed to be a welcome respite after WWII as well as celebrating the Centenary of the Great Exhibition of 1851 and celebrating the nation's past achievements in art, industry and science as well as looking to the future.

Pictured right:

1 William Street, Derby – where William and his family lived for a few years after WWII.
(It had stopped being used as a pub earlier).

William's military record ....

MILITARY RECORD FROM WWI: (National Archives adm/159/141 and adm/159/163)
Enlisted 4 August 1916 at Liverpool, born St Lukes, Derby, trade cook, religion Church of England.
Mother: Kathleen. Father: William – 20 Becket Well Lane, Derby.
On enlistment, as Private: 5' 6" tall, fresh complexion, grey eyes, light brown hair, scar on right buttock.
On final discharge from the service: 5'10" tall, fresh complexion etc

MILITARY RECORD:

Private E company	Recruit, depot Deal	4 August 1916 to 31 August 1916
	Character very good, ability: satisfactory. Commanding officer H. S. Neville	
	White. Services forfeited: Under-age 4 Aug 1916 to 5 March 1917, 214 days	
Private E company	1 Jan 1917 to 14 Feb 1917 – Transferred to Plymouth	
Private G company	15 Feb 1917 to 5 March 1917 Character very good, ability satisfactory,	
	Commanding officer: J C Edwards	
Private G company	6 March 1917 to 24 July 1917, cause of discharge: Embarked	
Private G company	Name of ship: "**HMS Colossus**" 25 July 1917 to 31 December 1917	
	Commander: C.F. Beatty POWNALL	
Private G company	Colossus 1 Jan 1918 to 31 Dec 1918	
Private G company	Plymouth Division 28 Jul 1919 to 20 Oct 1919. Embarked.	

There is a family story that William's ship was deployed near to St Petersburg at the time when
negotiations were taking place concerning the Romanovs (Russian Royal Family) and plans to
exile them to England, but the Bolsheviks murdered them before their exile took place (source: Sandra
PALMER – William's youngest daughter)

Private G company:	Name of ship: "**HMS Benbow**" 21 Oct 1919 to 31 Dec 1919.
	Commanding officer: C.D. CARPENDALE
Private G company:	Name of ship: "Benbow", 1 Jan 1920 to 31 Dec 1920, character very good,
	ability, satisfactory.
Private G company:	Name of ship: "**HMS Emperor of India**" 1 Apr 1921 to 10 Apr 1921
Private G company:	Plymouth Division:16 Apr 1921 to 30 June 1921. Cause of discharge R.M.B.m
Private G company:	1 Jul 1921 to 8 Oct 1921 , character very good, ability satisfactory,
Private G Company:	1 Jan 1922 to 14 Jan (or June) 1922. Discharged. Commanding officer: Mullins.
General character:	"Very good". Under-age from 4 Aug 1916 to 5 Mar 1917.
School certificates:	5 September 1916
Able to swim:	Yes
When tested:	18th October
Where tested:	Deal

Dates of passing and revision of drills: 12 Feb 1917, very good

Tested on musketry:	6 Jan 1917 passed
Field training:	10.4.1917 – very good
Tested on gunnery:	21 July 1917 – good

Wounds and hurts:

30 Aug 1919   – paid £17-8sh-8d

3 Aug 1920   – paid £6-13sh-1d

Second record of enlistment:

Date of enlistment: 18 September 1923

Occupation: bricklayer's labourer

Religion: Church of England

Father/Mother: William & Kathleen

On enlistment as a private: height 5' 9 ¼" tall, fresh complexion, light brown hair, grey eyes, no wounds or scars. Height at discharge 5' 10 1.4" tall

Rank: Marine, E company, at Chatham, Kent 1 Jan 1924 to 9 April 1924. **Discharged invalid.**** Character very good, ability satisfactory, commanding officer: Robertson F C EDWARDS
General character, very good, address see above.

Former service allowed: 4 years, 315 days.

Allowances 5 September 1916 – school certificates

Ability to swim: yes

When tested: 12 Oct 1916

Where: Deal

Wounds and hurts: 11 Jan 1924 - £1-6sh-6d – paid S.N.P.F.

Paid: War Gratuity, 30 August 1919 - £17-0-0.

** Footnote: There is a family story that William sustained a hand injury. So, it may be that this is the reference to "wounds and hurt" sustained by him on 11 Jan 1924. This would be during his period of second enlistment. A few weeks after this incident, he is discharged April 1924 – "Discharged invalid".

William's son Gordon PROUDLER recalls his father having numerous occupations over the years; from flower selling, working at the cattle market, painting/decorating and even, sometimes, working as an entertainer/comedian. William's wife had died in 1940 leaving him with a large family and young infant dependents. Therefore during WWII he "did his bit" locally whilst continuing to support his family. Although William is pictured earlier selling flowers, he also at this time worked for the Derbyshire Fire Service. He was also engaged for a time in work at the army base at Osmaston Road (close to present-day Ascot Drive fire station site). This was a large military base used by every corps of the army; facilities at the camp included a firing range and a large aircraft hangar where repairs to aircraft were carried out.

Marriage and Children .....

William's first marriage was to Lucy COLLOP (1901-1940) and they had six children:

William PROUDLER 1899-1986
married Lucy COLLOP 1901-40

Pam	Sheila	Brenda	Gordon	Roy	Barry
1926-2004	1927-2004	1929-2005	b.1932	b.1935	1937-2008

L to R: Sheila, Brenda and Pamela PROUDLER
Thanks to Sharon (Pamela's daughter) who supplied this picture
Estimated to have been taken about 2002
(abt 18 months before they all died)

Barry PROUDLER 1937-2008
Thanks to Gordon (brother)
who supplied this picture

Eldest daughter Pam PROUDLER 1926-2004 married several times and had 3 or 4 children. One of her sons was raised in America. She has many grandchildren today.
Sheila PROUDLER 1927-2004 married William HARGRAVES in 1946 in Derby. She had 2 or 3 children.
Brenda PROUDLER was born in 1929 in Derby and married Bill DEMPSEY about March 1947
also in Derby. They had four children and lived in Scotland.
Barry PROUDLER married Rose in about 1959 in Derby. They had four children. It is believed, at one time, he worked as a taxi driver. He is pictured (above) in his army uniform when he was doing National Service. During this time he was based in Germany.

Gordon PROUDLER (1932-living) -
Completed his National Service based in Scotland.
He is married with four children.

Roy PROUDLER (1935-living)
Completed National Service in Egypt.
He is married with a daughter & grandchildren

After his first wife's death in 1940, William marries, secondly to Lena Shaw on 19 September 1942 at Derby Registry Office. Lena was the daughter of BENJAMIN SHAW and ELIZABETH BROWN-GORDON. She was born October 28, 1913 in Lancashire, and died October 8, 2002 in Erewash, Derbyshire.

Lena already had two children from her previous marriage: Ralph and Sandra.

William and Lena have a daughter Sandra (b. 1943). Sandra marries Tom Palmer, son of Albert and Florence Palmer. Tom was a successful paraplegic athlete; winning the British Championship in 1962, a gold medal at the Empire Games in Perth, silver at the Tokyo Paraplegic Olympics in addition to being the World Paraplegic Weight-Lifting Champion.

Above, grave of William PROUDLER at Borrowash Cemetery. Says, in Loving Memory of a Dear Husband and Father WILLIAM PROUDLER, died 23.4.86 aged 87 years, R.I.P.

Grave space U32, burial rights purchased for 100 years. Grave located far corner. Enter the grave yard and, to the left, is a field of grave spaces and William is located in the far right corner. This is Borrowash Cemetery, which is different to the cemetery at Borrowash Church and is located a short distance away from the church, set back from the main road running through Borrowash. Second wife Lena PROUDLER (nee SHAW) is buried in the same location, grave space V32 – though we did not see an actual headstone for her, so perhaps both in the same grave.

Daughters of Bill and Kate

Doris Cecilia Proudler 1901-82

Doris (called Doll) was born July 1, 1901 in Derby and died 1982. She married WILLIAM HENRY (HARRY) ALLSOPP December 1921 in Derby. He was born June 28, 1903 in Derby, and died 1969 in Derby.

Doris Cecilia Proudler 1901-82 & Harry

William ALLSOPP, eldest son 1924-2004

Thanks to Betty (RYALLS) (nee HARTSHORN) and son-in-law Kevin POTTER for providing many of the photos on this branch of the family

Doris's husband, William Henry Allsopp (Harry) ran his own building company in Derby for many years ... Allsopp Builders – his company's main business was with the public house trade. His sons joined him in the business in due course and, following Harry's death in 1969, one of them continued the firm for some years. Harry, on occasions, provided work for his father-in-law, Bill PROUDLER 1874-1955 (bricklayer). Harry would set Bill on a job, but give him strict instructions not to climb ladders etc. But as soon as Harry was out of the way Bill would do exactly that.   Harry's business traded from buildings and land located right next door to the family home at 91 Uttoxeter Old Road. Doris continued to live at this address until her death in 1982. After their marriage in 1921, Doris and Harry set up home only yards away from the PROUDLERs, at the top of Becket Well Lane on Macklin Street – at Macklin Cottages.   Later, after WWII, they moved to Uttoxeter Old Road. Daughter Doris recalls, post-WWII, how the fields around this area were being worked by German and Italian prisoners-of-war.

Florence Beatrice 1903-88

Florence marries firstly Herbert HARTSHORN in Sept 1926 in Derby.
He died during WWII (but not of the conflict, he died of consumption -TB).
They have a daughter, Betty, later in 1926 and the family are to be found on
the 1933 electoral roll as being resident at 3 Becket Well Lane (her grandfather's house) where they lived for some time following Herbert's early

demise. The picture above is of Florence and is taken at Skegness by her husband Albert (2nd husband).
Kevin POTTER (husband of Florence's grand-daughter Brenda) tells how the couple always had the
professional street photographers take their photos.

*Thanks (again) to Betty Ryalls and Kevin
Potter for pictures and information on their
branch.*

Cecilia Proudler 1906-89

As a child, according to niece Brenda
HOLMES, Cissy dreamt of being a ballet
dancer – she could stand full on her toes
but, in fact – like her sisters, when she
was old enough was sent to work at
Rowleys Hosiery Factories on Uttoxeter
Old Road – the work strained her eyes
and she quickly had to wear glasses.
*Thank you to children Vera and Brian
HULME for this lovely picture.*
Cissy looks stunning.
Cissy married Joseph HULME who was
the manager of a pawnbrokers shop;
daughter Vera is born in Derby but they
lived for some time in Burton on Trent
where son Brian Joseph HULME was born.

They move to Derby about 1940 when father Joseph HULME is appointed manager of a pawnbrokers in
Regents Street Derby. Regent Street gets bombed in WWII and Brian recalls the area being cordoned off
and, when they did get access, how he picked up shrapnel in the pawn shop. (John Butlers
pawnbrokers). Joseph continued "pawnbroking" during WWII but "did his bit" by working in the
Auxiliary Fire Service for Derby.

Son Brian, during the 1950s, enlisted for military service with the RAF – Senior Aircraft Service 1955-57.
After initial training at Cardigan (Wales) he was stationed at RAF Stradishall (Suffolk) and RAF Chivenor
(Devon). During this period his unit was on stand-by for several weeks during the Suez Crisis, but were
stood down without engaging in active service. After military service Brian marries wife Ruth and later
has two daughters). Brian was employed for an impressive fifty years (which included his 3 years
military service) by Smith and Sons Master Clockmakers of Derby – who are still trading. He specialised
in repairing small clocks and, during his apprenticeship, spent three weeks at Chatsworth House learning
his trade. His work involved him in servicing clocks in a variety of premises around Derby.

Cissy's husband Joseph HULME in his later years, after he finishes working in the pawnbroker business,
latterly works at the Midland Drapery store in the carpet department. He dies in 1963 of cancer and,

after his death, Cissy sells the family home at 168 St Thomas's Road and lives for a time with sisters Florence and Dolly (Doris), before settling in Alvaston close to her son. She died of cancer.

Gladys Proudler 1909 - 1986

L to R: Gladys Proudler, husband Bill Smith and daughter Brenda

Gladys Proudler married Bill Smith in 1928. Bill was a barber at Wirksworth, Derbyshire for nearly 60 years, being the longest-serving businessman in the town. He lived with his family in a flat above the shop in the 3-storey building and began working in the business as a young 13-year old, sent out to work at Cowpes in St James Street, Derby. Initially tasked with general cleaning up, he developed an interest in hair-dressing and began learning the trade. He had to shave three balloons safely before being allowed to use the cut-throat razor on customers! Soon, customers began asking for "Ray" (his middle name was used as there was already a Bill in the shop). Then, when there was a vacancy for a manager at a Llandudno barber shop, he was asked if we would like to go and manage the shop for six months, which he did.

On how Gladys came to meet Bill, she would say that she went to visit him there (they had met when she was just 14 years old) and asked him "if you're so good, why don't you go on your own and work for yourself"? And that's exactly what he did. He started his own business and traded for 60 years. He charged 6 pence per hair cut, so had to do 40 hair cuts to make £1. He worked 8am till 7pm Monday to Friday and 8am till 10pm on a Saturday. Never had holidays, nor owned a car. Bill kept working into his eighties.

Brenda Holmes (nee SMITH), their daughter, during the 1960s was employed by Marks and Spencers and, on Saturdays, would walk around the Derby store modelling the different clothes that the store was selling for customers to see. After a few months of this, the store decided they were going to put on proper modelling shows all over the country and asked for volunteers from the staff to do this. No one volunteered, so the manager informed Brenda that she had "volunteered"! Brenda and a few others travelled around various venues, staying at top class hotels and the shows that were put on were

very professional The last of these shows in 1968 was back at Derby at the King's Hall. Brenda says ....
all the lights were on, flowers everywhere and the hall was absolutely packed. The Manager (Mr SMITH)
said, I think everyone here thinks that these girls are professional models? But then, to the audience's
absolute delight, we came out dressed in flat shoes and wearing our works overalls. Wow, did they
clap!!!

* * *

Lucy Proudler 1912-1993

Lucy marries Henry GREENSMITH in 1930 and has two children, Jean and Dennis.   She is included in the
group wedding photo below. Husband Henry (Harry) GREENSMITH dies young of meningitis. Later, she
secondly marries Henry's best friend Frank HARDWIDGE in 1937 and has another daughter Vera
HARDWIDGE, then later Tony HARDWIDGE, born 1948. Vera, in 1957, marries Allan J. ALLSOPP (Jimmy)
– this couple were first cousins. Allan J. ALLSOPP being the son of Doris Cecilia PROUDLER, born 1901.

Group Proudler Wedding Photograph

On the next page is a wedding photograph for Doris (junior's) (b.1933) wedding in 1952. That is, Doris
Allsopp (Doris jnr) who married Brian Kitching. Doris (jnr) being the daughter of Doris (or Doll) Proudler
who marries Harry Allsopp. So, basically, the bride is the grand-daughter of Bill and Kate Proudler. The
wedding party is shown in an upstairs room at the Scarsdale Arms public house on Colyear Street, Derby
which was only a few yards away from her grandparents' home and, of course, this was her
grandfather's local pub.

The picture shows Bill and Kate PROUDLER with 4 of their 7 children, 5 grandchildren and 2 great-
grandchildren. Children being: son Frank, daughters Lucy, Gladys and Doris; grandchildren being Betty
RYALLS, Joyce ALLSOPP, William ALLSOPP, Doris ALLSOPP, Vera HARDWIDGE; great-grandchildren being
Brenda RYALLS and Jeffrey WOOLLEY.

From left to right – back row: Bill ALLSOPP, Gladys ALLSOPP, Brenda RYALLS (baby), Jack RYALLS, Betty
RYALLS, Joyce ALLSOPP, Hazel (Fred's wife), Nella (Jack's wife), Roy WOOLLEY, Jeffrey WOOLLEY, Muriel
(Bill's wife) ... the rest are KITCHING relatives.

From left to right - Middle/front rows. Seated lady farthest left is Kate PROUDLER (1875-1957), standing
immediately behind her is her husband William (Bill) PROUDLER (1874-1955); to his right on the front
row there is David Frank PROUDLER (1897-1966) and his wife Dorothy (1900-1997). To their right is Lucy
PROUDLER, next three unknown, then Harry ALLSOPP, Doris ALLSOPP (bride's mother), Brian KITCHING
(groom), Doris ALLSOPP (jnr) (bride), next unknown, then Brian KITCHING's father (groom's father), next
few unknown, then young girl 2nd from right is Vera ALLSOPP (nee HARDWIDGE) Lucy PROUDLER's
daughter, end right unknown.

DERBY PROUDLERS GROUP WEDDING PHOTO 1952

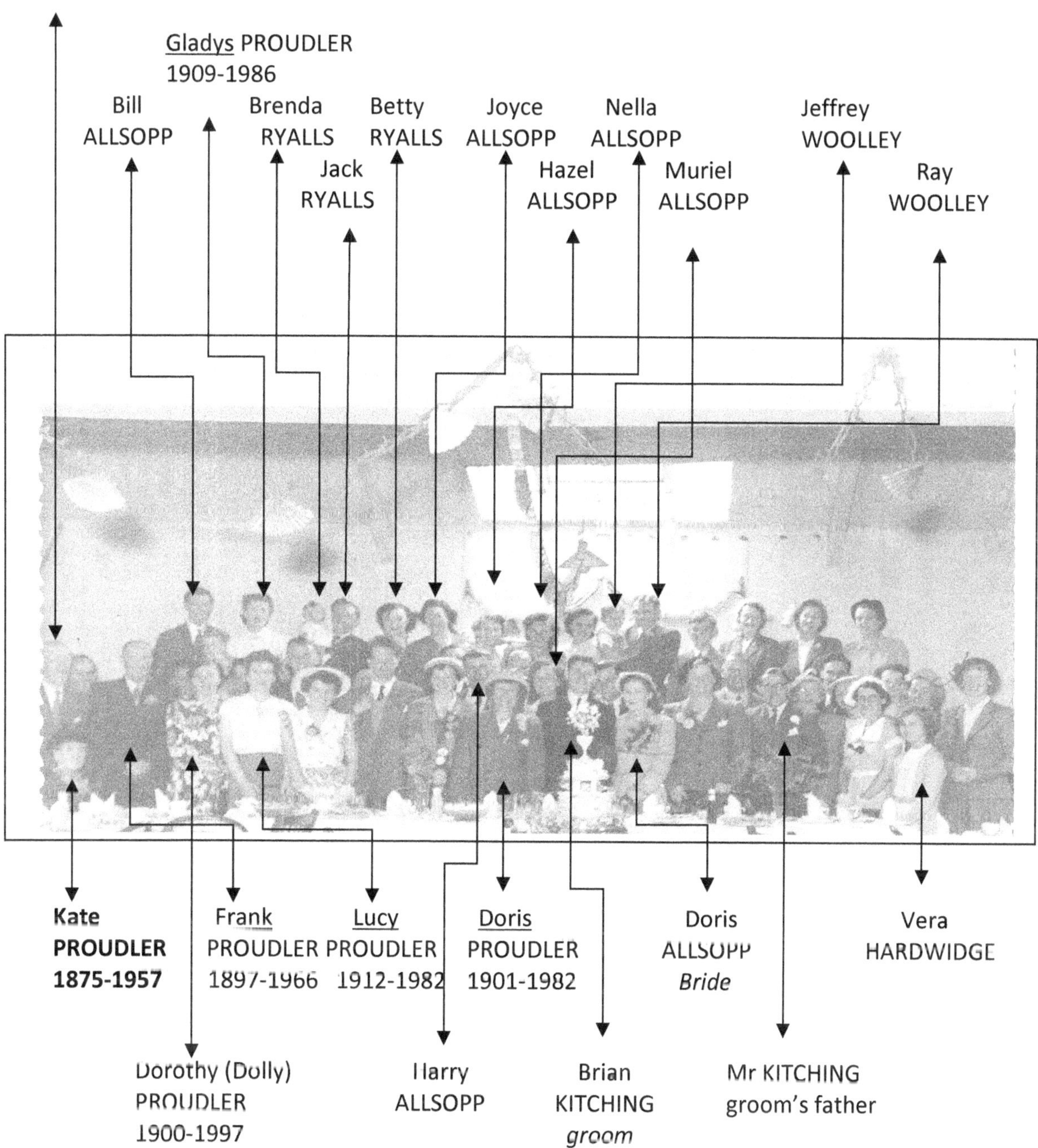

Many of the family members to the right of the bride in the picture are the KITCHING family, except for the young girl, front row on the right (shortest female) – this is Lucy PROUDLER's daughter Vera, who later marries her first cousin Jim ALLSOPP, the bride's youngest brother.

Doris recalls that her Aunt Florence was not on her wedding photo – as she was probably courting Albert Edward BRADBURY (who lived next door to the PROUDLERs). Florence used to give her bottles to take in order to get admission to the pictures. The Empire picture house was also close to the family home and parents sometimes used to try and sneak their little ones inside when no-one was watching.

Doris, along with her cousin Brenda HOLMES (nee Smith) worked for a time on Colyear Street, Derby – Doris would pop round to her grandmother's (Kate PROUDLER) every day for lunch.

Husband Brian KITCHING served as Chief Petty Officer in the Navy during the 1950s, not just for National Service, as Brian signed up for a seven year period and travelled the world during this time. For a time he was stationed at British Guiana.

SHROPSHIRE PROUDLERS TO PRESENT

Very few people with the Proudler name remained in the home county - the largest branches thrived away from Shropshire. Those who remained stayed in the area which has, today, been completely built over and developed as Telford New Town (3rd wave of English New Towns, created 1968) - a town that calls itself "The Birthplace of Industry".

Present-day Proudlers in America descend from this branch. James John Proudler 1879-1973 married Mary Ann Parry and this couple sail to America in 1910 settling initially in Erie. Today there are some 5 generations of descendants from this couple.

Descendants of John Proudler

1 John Proudler b: May 10, 1829 in Priorslee, Shifnal, Shropshire d: 1919 in Newport, Shropshire
.. +Martha Rider b: 1842 in Lilleshall m: December 1860 in Shifnal, Shropshire d: Abt. 1882 in Salop
.... 2 Elizabeth Proudler b: 1861 d: 1864 in Wellington, Shropshire
.... 2 John Henry Proudler b: 1864 d: April 2, 1928
...........+Annie Smith b: 1862 m: March 1886 in Newport, Shropshire d: April 2, 1928
.... 3 Martha Proudler b: 1884 in Shifnal, Shropshire
.......................+William John Robinson b: 1881 in Wellington, Shropshire m: June 1905 in Newport, Shropshire
............................4 Frances Vivian Robinson b: 1908
............................4 Annie Elizabeth Robinson b: 1908
............................4 William John Robinson b: 1910
............................4 Martha Robinson b: 1911
............................4 Alfred Robinson b: 1913
............................4 Adelaide M. Robinson   b: 1916
............................4 Horace Robinson b: 1919
............................4 Reginald J. Robinson b: 1922
............................4 Kenneth Robinson b: 1926
............................4 Clifford Robinson b: 1928
...................3 James Proudler b: 1887
.......................+? m: December 1908 in Wellington, Shropshire
...................3 John Henry Proudler b: 1887 d: 1894 in Shifnal
...................3 Thomas Proudler b: 1888 d: 1889 in Newport, Shropshire
...................3 Annie Proudler b: 1890 d: 1894 in Newport, Shropshire
...................3 Polly Proudler b: 1891 in Newport, Shropshire
...........................4 Annie Proudler b: 1912 in Madeley, Shropshire d: 2006
.............................+Albert E. Hampton m: June 1933 in Madeley
...........................4 George V.G. Proudler b: 1919
.... 3 Richard Leonard Proudler b: 1892 d: June 1893 in Newport, Shropshire
...................3 Maria Proudler b: 1893 in Shifnal, Shropshire
.... +George Gwilliam m: July 1920 in Shifnal, Shropshire
...........................4 Gordon J. Gwilliam b: May 1921 in Shifnal, Salop
.... 3 William Proudler b: 1896 in St Georges, Shifnal d: May 3, 1973
.... |Edith Mindham b: 1893 m: March 1920 in Newport, Shropshire d: 1981
...........................4 John James Proudler b: July 10, 1921 in Ketley Bank, Shropshire d: March 2009 in Ketley Bank, Shropshire
.... |Doris Merrington b: Abt. 1928 in Ketley Bank, Shropshire m: March 1951 in Wellington, Shropshire
..................................5 Anthony John Proudler b: July 14, 1958
.... 4 Derick Robert John Proudler b: 1928 d: November 1987
.... +Ann Howells m: December 1955 in Wellington, Shropshire
.... 3 Emily Proudler b: 1899 in Shifnal, Shropshire
.... +James A. Pidgeon m: November 1919 in Newport, Salop
.... 4 Noel J. Pidgeon b: November 1921 in Newport, Salop
        2 Mary Elizabeth Proudler b: 1866
            3 Ben Jacks Proudler b: 1886
.... +Kate Withington m: December 1917 in Shifnal, Shropshire
...........................4 Thomas J Jacks b: 1919 in St Asaph, Wales
...........................4 Mary K C Jacks b: 1922 in St Asaph, Wales
.... *2nd Husband of Mary Elizabeth Proudler:
...........+Thomas Jacks b: 1864 m: June 1889 in Wellington, Shropshire
...................3 Joseph Herbert Jacks b: 1890
.... 3 Martha Jacks b: 1891
.... 3 Hilda Jacks b: 1893 in Wellington, Shropshire
.... 3 James Jacks b: 1902 in Ormskirk, Lancashire

.... 2 Martha Proudler (aka Patricia) b: 1867 in Shifnal, Shropshire d: 1909 in Shropshire
..........+Thomas Finlayson b: 1869 in Newport, Salop   m: 1891 in Newport, Shropshire d: Aft. 1911
.................3 Martha Ellen Elizabeth Finlayson (aka Nellie) b: 1892 d: August 14, 1958 in Isolation Hospital, Ilford, Essex
.... +Arthur Pownall
...........................4 Patricia Pownall b: Abt. 1914
.... +Frederick Kemp
...............................5 Peter Kemp b: 1936
...............................5 Kenneth Kemp b: 1940 d: 1962
...............................4 Megan Pownall b: Abt. 1915
.... +William Hames
................................5 Christine Hames   b: Abt. 1948
...........................4 Nellie Pownall b: January 4, 1916
.... +Albert Clarke b: December 11, 1916 m: May 1940 in Middlesex
.... 5 Gwenneth P Clark b: April 28, 1946 in Poplar, Middlesex
...............................+Alan J Whiteside m: May 1973 in Thurrock, Essex d: 2009
...............................6 Lindsey Anne M Whiteside b: 1975 in Thurrock
....................................+John
.... *2nd Husband of Lindsey Anne M Whiteside:
.....................................7 Rachel ? b: May 22, 1992
.... 6 Karen Whiteside b: Abt. 1977
.....................................7 Michael ? b: January 15, 2000
.... 6 Alexander Whiteside b: Abt. 1979
...................4 William Arthur Pownall b: Abt. 1918
...................+Olive Gauldthorpe
...........................5 Stephen Pownall   b: 1948
...........................5 Linda Pownall b: Abt. 1949
.................*2nd Husband of Martha Ellen Elizabeth Finlayson (aka Nellie):
......................+Frederick Gauldthorpe m: Abt. 1930
.... 2 Thomas Proudler b: 1873 in Wellington, St Georges d: 1929
..........+? m: December 1897 in Wellington, Shropshire
.... 3 Elsie Proudler b: 1898 in Wellington, Shropshire d: 1898 in Wellington, Shropshire
.................3 Ernest Proudler b: 1902 d: 1902 in Wellington, Shropshire
.... 3 Thomas Proudler   b: 1903 d: 1903
.... 2 Maria Proudler b: 1877 in Shifnal d: Aft. 1951 in Shropshire
..........+Joseph Morris b: 1877 m: June 1901 in Newport, Shropshire d: Aft. 1951 in Shropshire
.................3 May Morris b: 1903
..................+? Jones
...........................4 Gwen Jones b: Abt. 1926
..........................+James Jones
.................3 Elsie Morris b: 1906
.... 2 James John Proudler b: September 12, 1879 in Wellington, Salop d: August 1973 in USA
..........+Mary Ann Parry b: 1883 in Wellington, Salop   m: October 24, 1908 in Wellington, Shropshire d: Aft. 1958 in USA
.................3 John James Proudler b: 1914 in Erie, Pennsylvania USA d: August 27, 2008 in Florida, USA
......................+Mary Sperry b: July 13, 1916 in Erie, Pennsylvania USA d: July 4, 1976 in Erie, Pennsylvania USA
.... 4 Thomas James Proudler b: 1946 in Erie, Pennsylvania USA
.... +Lynn Becker b: 1946 in Erie, Pennsylvania USA
...........................5 Laura Renee Proudler b: October 25, 1968
.... +Michael John Tate
...............................6 Chelsey Lynn Tate b: November 12, 1993
...............................6 Meghan McDevitt Tate b: October 14, 1995
...............................6 Gavin Michael Tate b: November 2, 1998
...........................5 Jeffery Thomas Proudler b: 1970
............................+Colleen C. Quish m: in Fairfield, Connecticut, USA
...........................4 Patrick John Proudler b: 1950 in Erie, Pennsylvania USA
.............................+Linda b: 1948 in Erie, Pennsylvania USA
...........................5 Jason Patrick Proudler b: 1976
.... +Hannah
...............................6 Elias Jason Proudler   b: April 2007
...........................5 Joshua John Proudler b: 1978
............................+Chisato
...............................6 Zion Proudler b: August 2006
...............................6 Ciarra Eve Proudler   b: March 17, 2009 in Minnesota, USA
         *2nd Wife of John Proudler:
..+Emma b: 1851m: March 1884 in Wellington, Shropshire
.... 2 Betsy Ann Proudler b: 1884 in Lodge Wood, Salop
..........+Joseph Corf m: 1907 in Ruthin, Denbighshire
.................3 Wilfred Joseph Corf b: 1908 in Ruthin, Denbighshire
.................3 Mildred Annie Corf b: 1910 in Aughton, Lancs
......................+George Sunderland m: 1937 in Ormskirk
.................3 Ronald J Corf b: 1912 in Ormskirk, Lancashire

APPENDIX 1

SHROPSHIRE PARISH RECORDS
Lichfield Diocese, Vol. XX. HIGH ERCALL
PROUDLEY (Prowder and PROWDLEY)

p. 217	5 June 1682	Marriage	Richardus PROWDLEY et Maria CHIRME, de Walton pactum conjugale fecere
p. 220	15 Apr 1683	Baptism of Richardus	Son of Richardi PROWDLEY de Walton et Mariae
p. 230	25 Oct 1685	Baptism of Johannes	Daughter of Richardi PROWDLY PROWDLEY de Walton, et Mariae
p. 239	19 Nov 1688	Baptism of Thomas	Son of Richardi PROWDLEY de Walton et Mariae
p. 247	[blank] 1691	Baptism of Samuel	Son of Richardi PROWDLEY de Walton et Mariae
p. 259	1 May 1695	Burial of Richardus	Richardus PROUDLEY de Walton
p. 267	27 Jan 1697	Marriage	Gulielmus Teese et Maria PROUDLEY, vidua, de Walton, de Clubb, Matrimonio jungebantur
p. 273	10 Aug 1699	Burial (Sepultus)	Of Samuel PROUDLEY (son of Richardi et Mariae)
p. 319	1 June 1713	Marriage	John PROUDLEY and Ann Haseldine
p. 320	17 Nov 1713	Baptism of Thomas	Son of Thomas PROUDLEY of Walton of the Club and Sarah.
p. 322	8 Apr 1714	Baptism of Anne	Daughter of John PROUDLEY of Walton and Anne
p. 331	25 Nov 1716	Baptism of John	Son of John PROUDLEY of Walton of the Club and Anne
p. 334	29 Sep 1717	Baptism of Edward	Son of Thomas and Sarah PROUDLEY of Walton
p. 343	10 Apr 1720	Baptism of Sarah	Daughter of Thomas PROUDLEY and Sarah of Walton
p. 343	3 July 1720	Baptism of Peter	Son of John PROUDLEY and Anne of Walton
p. 348	29 Apr 1722	Baptism of Mary	Daughter of Thomas PROUDLEY and Sarah
p. 362	23 Oct 1726	Baptism of William	Son of Thomas PROUDLEY of Walton and Sarah
p. 372	20 June 1729	Burial of William	Son of Thomas PROUDLEY of Walton
p. 373	22 Aug 1729	Burial of Ann	Wife of John PROUDLEY
p. 376	14 Apr 1730	Burial of John	John PROUDLEY in the township of Walton
p. 392	11 Dec 1735	Burial of Thomas	Son of Thomas PROUDLEY of Walton and Sarah
p. 398	7 Feb 1738	Baptism of Ann	Daughter of John PROUDLEY of The Oak
p. 405	29 Jan 1741	Baptism of Christian	Daughter of John PROUDLEY of Walton
p. 405	27 Feb 1741	Burial of Elizabeth	Daughter of John PROUDLEY of The Oak, Walton
p. 407	14 Sept 1741	Marriage	Andrew Picken and Sarah PROUDLEY

p. 410	6 Mar 1743	Burial of John	John PROUDLEY of t. Of Walton.
p. 412	20 Nov 1743	Baptism of Elizabeth	Daughter of the widow, PROUDLEY of The Oak, t. Of Walton
p. 416	2 Oct 1745	Marriage	Peter PROUDLEY and Elizabeth Talbott
p. 435	26 Dec 1751	Marriage	Edward PROUDLEY and Mary Turner
p. 440	12 June 1753	Baptism of Edward	Son of Edward PROUDLEY of Walton
p. 444	29 Nov 1754	Baptism of Mary	Daughter of Edward PROUDLEY of Walton
p. 455	17 Jan 1759	Burial of Sarah	Wife of Thomas PROUDLEY of Walton
p. 478	5 May 1766	Burial of Thomas	Thomas PROUDLEY (an 'ospital man) [this is as written]
p. 494	12 June 1771	Burial of Mary	Wife of Edward PROUDLEY of Walton
p. 514	10 July 1778	Burial of Edward	Edward PROUDLEY of Walton
p. 635	12 Aug 1782	Marriage	John Humphryes and Mary PROWDLEY. Witnesses: Richard Humphryes and Wm Robinson
p. 530	28 Dec 1783	Baptism of Thomas	Son of Edward PROUDLEY of Walton
p. 565	11 June 1793	Baptism of James	Son of Edward PROUDLEY of Walton
p. 661	26 Jan 1815	Marriage	Thomas PROUDLEY and Elizabeth Evason. Witnesses: Edward PROUDLEY and Mary Evason.

Parish Registers – St Chad's, Shropshire

Marriage of Christian (or Christiana) PROUDLEY to Thomas PICKEN, 8 July 1766.
Burial of Edward PROUDLEY, aged 19, on 24 July 1791.
Marriage of Thomas PROUDLEY to Sarah Rodenhurst both of Ercol Magna on 22 Sept 1712.

APPENDIX 2

PARISH REGISTER FOR LONGFORD-BY-NEWPORT

On microfiche (no. 4), Longford Register Sept 1741-1787

| 1750 | Richard, the son of Peter and Elizabeth PROUDLOW was baptised February 2nd. |

SHROPSHIRE PARISH RECORDS
Lichfield Diocese, Vol. III, Wrockwardine
PROUDLER (Proudle, PROUDLEY, PROWDLEY, Prowley)

p. 184	3 Nov 1754	Baptism of Ann	Daughter of Peter PROWDLEY and Elizabeth
p. 229	16 Mar 1783	Baptism of Richard	Son of Richard PROWDLEY and Ann
p. 180	3 May 1752	Baptism of Elizabeth	Daughter of Peter PROWLEY and Elizabeth
p. 185	3 June 1755	Burial of Thomas	Son of Peter PROWDLEY and Elizabeth
p. 196	7 Apr 1763	Burial of Mary	Daughter of Peter PROWDLEY and Elizabeth
p. 225	24 Aug 1780	Burial of Elizabeth	Wife of Peter PROUDLER (age 59)
p. 305	12 July 1807	Marriage	Richard PROUDLEY and Elizabeth MANNERING (signs Proudle)
p. 264	6 Sept 1805	Burial of John	John PROUDLER, age 59.
p. 231	3 Apr 1785	Burial of Peter	Peter PROUDLER, age 65.

Roddington Parish Registers
Baptism of Mary daughter of John PROUDLEY and Anne, page 1, in July 1678
Baptism of Richard, son of John PROUDLEY and Anne, page 3, 1681 Apr 18
Baptism of John, son of John PROUDLEY and Anne, page 8, 1689 Apr 4
Baptism of Elizabeth, daughter of Richard PROUDLEY [yeoman] and Elizabeth, page 18, 1704 Feb 2
Burial of John, son of John PROUDLEY [yeoman] and Elizabeth (error? Possibly Anne) Affit made June 21, page 19, 1708 June 13
Baptism of John, son of Richard PROUDLEY and Elizabeth, page 19, 1708 June 27
Burial of John PROUDLEY, PAGE 21 1701, Feb 7
Burial of Anne PROUDLEY, Feb 11 1710 affit for both 12th Feb.
Baptism of Anne daughter of Richard PROUDLEY and Elizabeth, page 23 1714 28th August
Roddington is 3 miles north-east of Wrockwardine.

APPENDIX 4

Extracted from Settlement Examinations – Poor Law Relief

Transcribed by members of the North East Telford Studies Group

P316/L/8/93 Dec 03 1783

Examination of Richard PROUDLOW (X), age 30, wife Ann. Children Jane 5, Elizabeth 3, Richard inf.
Born Pave Lane, Longford, Salop, lives in Wrockwardine Wood. High Ercall his father's parish.

SOURCES

Birth Certificates:

Birth Certificate for Maria PROUDLER 1843
Birth Certificate for Thomas PROUDLER 1846
Birth Certificate for George PROUDLER, 1855
Birth Certificate for Thomas PROUDLER, 1888
Birth Certificate for James PROUDLER, 1879
Birth Certificate for Francis Albert PROUDLER, 1897
Birth Certificate for Agnes Eveline PROUDLER, 1895
Birth Certificate for Thomas Ivan PROUDLER, 1899
Birth Certificate for Albert PROUDLER, 1867
Birth Certificate for Thomas PROUDLER, 1841
Birth Certificate for Agnes PROUDLER, 1864
Birth Certificate for Dorothy May Cordelia PROUDLER, 1901
Birth Certificate for Richard PROUDLER, 1845
Birth Certificate for Phoebe PROUDLER, 1871
Birth Certificate for Frederick PROUDLER, 1890-1960
Birth Certificate for Marian Florence PROUDLER, 1913
Birth Certificate for Florence Emma PROUDLER, 1884
Birth Certificate for John PROUDLER, 1852
Birth Certificate for Lucy PROUDLER 1893
Birth Certificate for David PROUDLER 1852-1927
Birth Certificate Michael PROUDLER 1945-
Birth Certificate for William PROUDLER 1874-1955
Birth Certificate David Frank PROUDLER 1897-1966
Birth Certificate for Tom PALMER
Birth Certificate for Sandra PALMER/PROUDLER
Birth Certificate for William PROUDLER
Birth Certificate for Pamela PROUDLER (b. 1926-)
Birth Certificate for David Leslie PROUDLER (b. 1944)
Birth Certificate for Florence Beatrice PROUDLER 1903
Birth Certificate for Robert Herbert HARTSHORN 1903
Birth Certificate for Betty HARTSHORN 1926
Birth Certificate Roy PROUDLER, 1932 (Derby)

Marriage Certificates:

Marriage Certificate for Albert PROUDLER, 1893
Marriage Certificate for Florence Emma PROUDLER, 1939
Marriage Certificate for Thomas PROUDLER, 1902
Marriage Certificate for Thomas PROUDLER, 1851
Marriage Certificate for Phoebe PROUDLER, 1895
Marriage Certificate for Martha PROUDLER (aka Pattie), 1902
Marriage Certificate for Thomas PROUDLER, 1862
Marriage Certificate for John PROUDLER, 1857
Marriage Certificate for Thomas PROUDLER, 1898
Marriage Certificate for David F PROUDLER, 1981
Marriage Certificate for Karen and Graham PROUDLER

Marriage Certificate for Laura PROUDLER 1942
Marriage Certificate for Sarah PROUDLER 1855
Marriage Certificate for Sandra PALMER/PROUDLER
Marriage Certificate for William PROUDLER /Lena SHAW
Marriage Certificate for Sheila PROUDLER
Marriage Certificate for Michael PROUDLER, 1980
Marriage Certificate for William PROUDLER 1874 / C MERRIN
Marriage Certificate for Florence HARTSHORN

Death Certificates:

Death Certificate for Joseph PROUDLER 1762-1840
Death Certificate for Annie May PROUDLER 1888-1978
Death Certificate for Frederick PROUDLER, 1891-1960
Death Certificate for John PROUDLER, 1829-1919
Death Certificate for Iris M. PROUDLER, 1915
Death Certificate for Elsie May PROUDLER, 1912
Death Certificate for Margaret PROUDLER, 1922
Death Certificate for David Frank PROUDLER 1966
Death Certificate for William PROUDLER 1955
Death Certificate for David PROUDLER 1927
Death Certificate for Lena PROUDLER 1913-2002
Death Certificate for Lucie PROUDLER 1901–1940
Death Certificate for Laura PROUDLER 1997
Death Certificate for Ann MERRIN 1883

Census Returns:

Census (1841) – Shropshire Martha
Census (1841) – Shropshire (original)
Census (1841) – Shropshire (printed)
Census (1851) – Shropshire (original)
Census (1851) – Shropshire (printed)
Census (1861) – Shropshire (original)
Census (1861) – Shropshire (printed)
Census (1871) – Shropshire (original)
Census (1871) – Shropshire (printed)
Census (1881) – Shropshire/Staffs/Yorks
Census (1891) – Derby
Census (1901) – Derby
Census (1911) – Shropshire (original)
Census (1911) – Derby [William] (original)
Census (1911) – Derby [David] (printed)

9 780956 683113